To Paul Lucas

Thank you for your confidence and encouragement
over the years

John Delay   20/11/88.

ASBESTOS REMOVAL, MANAGEMENT AND CONTROL

Asbestos Removal, Management and Control

John Delaine, Dip.Chem.Eng,
C.Eng, FI Chem.E, M.Inst.E,
MIWEM MIOSH

Gower Technical

Published by
Gower Technical
Gower Publishing Company Ltd,
Gower House,
Croft Road,
Aldershot,
Hants GU11 3HR,
England

Gower Publishing Company,
Old Post Road,
Brookfield,
Vermont 05036,
U.S.A.

British Library Cataloguing in Publication Data
Delaine, John
 Asbestos removal, management and control.
 1. Asbestos materials. Removal. Safety measures
 I. Title
 363.1'79

ISBN 0 566 09000 7

Printed and bound in Great Britain by
Anchor Brendon Ltd, Tiptree, Essex

Contents

Illustrations

Figures

Tables

Plates

Introduction

Since the mid-1970s asbestos removal has become an important aspect of work in the construction industry.

The widespread use of this naturally occurring fibrous mineral in the 1950s and 1960s for insulation, fireproofing and structural purposes means that asbestos-containing materials will be encountered in almost every refurbishment or demolition project. Its use as insulation for steam and heating systems necessitates removal prior to repairs or modernization.

Medical evidence gathered over many years has shown that exposure to the material is hazardous to health and leads to unfortunate health effects, which have a development period of 10-30 years, thus evidence is slow to collect. If not correctly handled, considerable quantities of asbestos dust will be released and there have been many press reports of such incidents. Whether these have been due to lack of knowledge, or lack of desire to carry out the handling procedures correctly is not clear.

However, at the time of preparation of this book, a major revision of legislation is being put together which will be likely to set the scene for some years to come. This will bring all aspects of the work under the control of the Health and Safety at Work etc. Act 1974 and remove present anomalies. Legislation since 1980 has introduced the requirements for specifications to handle asbestos, whether they be contractors, analysts or administrators, i.e. 'the architect or the engineer'.

The book attempts to give an overview on the subject to all sections of the asbestos industry and to set out the basis of good practice for those not in day-to-day contact with the subject. It should also form the basis of an initial appreciation for the intending specialist who will, no doubt, wish to consult additional reading matter from the bibliography provided.

Chapter 1

OCCURRENCE, PROPERTIES AND USES

In recent years the word 'asbestos' has been used with some trepidation as one of the potential major hazards of the time. As with many other hazards it has provoked hysterical reaction in people's minds, whereas only 15–20 years ago it was being used as a wonder material. However, whatever viewpoint is taken, work with asbestos is now tightly controlled and its wide usage means that almost all maintenance, refurbishment and demolition work is influenced by its presence.

It is hoped that this book will demonstrate the care which is taken and the reasons for such procedures, also that it will give a readable account of the development of the controls now applied.

First it is important to understand what asbestos is and how it has been used and, in fact, is being used. There are a number of misconceptions which have arisen from 'little knowledge'.

Asbestos is defined in the Oxford Dictionary as:

- the unquenchable stone;
- incombustible flax;
- a mineral of fibrous structure capable of being woven into incombustible fabric.

Encyclopaedias explain the subject generally in the following terms.

Asbestos is not, as many people think, made from vegetable fibre, but is the general name for the useful fibrous variety of a number of rock-forming minerals. The fibres may be spun or felted to make fabrics, panels and coatings that are resistant to heat and chemical action. It is also valued for its electrical insulating properties.

Historically, asbestos was known in ancient times. Pliny the Elder describes shrouds of woven asbestos used in the cremation of the nobility. Other writers of the time describe lamp wicks which were not consumed by the flame and which were used in the temples of the Vestal Virgins.

The Emperor Charlemagne is fabled to have amazed guests by throwing an asbestos table cloth on to the fire to be cleaned and Marco Polo is reported to have seen asbestos cloth in Central Asia.

Nevertheless, asbestos had little commercial use until the late nineteenth century when mining began in Italy and Canada. The latter led to the development of the town of Asbestos in Quebec Province whose main industry is the quarrying and processing of the igneous rock deposits for the asbestos fibre.

The substance results from chemical action on the rocks which years ago caused the deposit to change its form and to swell into a stiff clay-like substance containing a large proportion of water. As the water evaporated the material dried leaving cracks and crevices which it is thought contained spores and seeds which remained trapped within the rock. These then formed the basis for the fibre growth as part of the rock.

The rock is mined in the same way as other minerals such as iron and copper and is also found as an impurity contaminating hard rock gold mines, vermiculite and talc.

The term was originally applied only to fine amphibole varieties and is retained in commercial usage even though 95 per cent of the asbestos now used is prepared from serpentine rocks.

Types of asbestos

The mineral occurs as six major types which are split into amphibole and serpentine groups according to their physical and chemical properties:

Amphibole	Serpentine
Crocidolite –blue asbestos	Chrysotile –white asbestos
Amosite –brown asbestos	
Anthophyllite	
Tremolite	
Actinolite	

Of these, only chrysotile, crocidolite and amosite are regularly found in commercial use in the UK, although traces of the remaining three types may occasionally occur.

Amphiboles

Crocidolite is a sodium, iron amphibole $Na_2O_3.FeO.Fe_2O_3.8SiO_2.H_2O$. It is also known as blue asbestos because of its dull blue colour. Its fibres are of high tensile strength, and it is resistant to corrosion, but it fuses at relatively low temperatures.

Amosite is a magnesium iron silicate, closely related to anthophyllite of formula $(FeO.MgO)SiO_2.H_2O$. It has a high bulk density and the fibres possess a springiness with a considerable resistance to corrosion. The name is reported to derive from the initial letters of its occurrence at Asbestos Mines of South Africa.

Anthophyllite is a magnesium iron silicate with lower iron content than amosite.

Tremolite   is a calcium magnesium silicate and actinolite
                 results from the substitution of part of the
                 magnesium with iron.

Serpentines

Chrysotile   is a hydrated magnesium silicate
                 $2SiO_2.3MgO.2H_2O$. It makes up about 95 per cent
                 of all asbestos and is commercially the most
                 important variety of the mineral. The fibres are
                 superior in length, flexibility, fineness and
                 tensile strength to other varieties. Chrysotile is
                 less acid resistant than the amphiboles and
                 subject to progressive embrittlement on
                 exposure to temperatures above $400–500°C$.
                 However, its availability permits it to dominate
                 the market.

Occurrence of asbestos deposits

Asbestos in one or other of its forms occurs in many areas of
the world where it is mined for commercial use.

First reports of commercial extraction refer to an Italian mine
in 1868 and, with the discovery of large-scale deposits in
Quebec, Canada at about the same time.

Other sources listed include South Africa, USSR, USA, Brazil,
Cyprus, Japan, Austria, France, Bolivia, China, Yugoslavia,
Finland and India.

Exploitation of these deposits grew rapidly with the growth of
construction and utilization of energy sources in the
industrialized world. The properties of fire resistance, non-
conductivity of heat and electricity and the ability of the fibre to
provide a binder to cement, plaster etc., all combined to make
such growth.

Production of asbestos fibre increased dramatically during the 1960s and 1970s (see Table 1.1) with by far the largest production occurring in the USSR and Canada.

Table 1.1

Increase in production, 1960-1976		
to	1930	below	5000 x 10^6 Kg
	1960		2210
	1970		3490
	1973		4093
	1974		4115
	1975		4560
	1976		5178

Source: *WHO Asbestos,* 1 ARC, vol. 14, 1979, p.29.

Uses of asbestos

Asbestos fibres have been used in an extremely wide variety of situations in building and industry. The main areas are listed in the following paragraphs.

Asbestos cement

This is now the principal area of use for asbestos. Generally the fibre is present as chrysotile although older asbestos cement products may contain crocidolite and, in specific items such as ceiling tiles, amosite.

The products are based on the addition of asbestos fibres (around 10-15 per cent by weight) to a non-combustible filler such as Portland cement. Asbestos cement is typically a high-compression, high-density, hard-surfaced material which is commonly employed for fire protection panels, corrugated panels for roofing and cladding, roof tiles, fire surrounds, rainwater goods, water tanks and water pipework etc.

Asbestos insulation board

This product is similar to the hard-surfaced asbestos cement, but has a higher asbestos content (up to 40 per cent). The fibre is often present as amosite. Occasionally 1-2 per cent of crocidolite is also found. The material is mainly used as a lightweight cladding for walls, ceilings and structural steelwork and for acoustic and thermal insulation as well as fire protection.

Asbestos lagging

Asbestos fibres have been widely used in the preparation of insulation for vessels and pipework in heat and steam-raising plant, and for reaction vessels and furnaces in industry. The fibre content varies considerably but is generally in the range 5–55 per cent. In a number of instances however preformed sections will be found with over 80 per cent fibre content – amosite and crocidolite have been experienced in this area.

In general, however, the asbestos fibres which may include any or all of the main types were mixed with a plaster/cement base and wrapped or moulded round the pipework or vessel.

The properties of the various types often dictate their point of use which will be discussed later.

Sprayed asbestos

Sprayed asbestos comprises a mixture of up to 85-90 per cent of any type of asbestos bound with cement. The product was applied, as the name suggests, by spray gun but is no longer accepted for use. The main advantage was for insulation or fibre protection problems when surfaces were large, uneven or awkwardly shaped.

The areas of use therefore were on structural steel, ceilings and walls for visual effect, sound attenuation and fire protection.

However, due to the often rapid degradation of the mixture and consequent emission of fibres, its use diminished.

Up to around 1970 any of the three main types of asbestos may have been used in layers from one-half to almost two inches thick and no sprayed coatings have been applied since 1984.

Woven asbestos and rope

This, along with sprayed asbestos, is potentially one of the most hazardous products, often containing in excess of 90 per cent asbestos in a loose friable form.

Woven asbestos has been used to form the covers of quilts which were then filled with loose fibres for insulation purposes. Asbestos fire blankets remain in evidence in many situations and asbestos ropes or caulking were manufactured for many and various purposes where flexible jointing was required.

Jointings and packings

In these products, the fibres, principally chrysotile in the range 30-80 per cent, were mixed with a variety of materials to form plugs or fillers and gaskets for sealing ovens, engine parts or sections of system-built buildings.

Friction products

Most brake and clutch linings did, and many still do, contain asbestos, the use being widespread in road vehicles, trains, lifts and other machinery. Chrysotile at 30-70 per cent is moulded with fillers and phenolic resins to make the linings. The fibres give rigidity and maintain structural properties at high temperatures. Due to the temperature which can be generated, the asbestos fibres can break down to non-fibrous silicates which are at present considered non-hazardous. However, this does not mean that the dust created in use necessarily contains no asbestos.

Paints, paper, floor coverings etc.

Asbestos fibres have been used in paints to provide decorative, lumpy finishes and to provide added strength and cohesion. Alternatives for this use have been relatively simple to develop. Similarly, asbestos paper and the inclusion as a filler in floor coverings have been replaced by alternatives in recent years.

Chapter 2

EXPOSURE
AND HEALTH

Association with health effects

Exposure to asbestos dust, both from occupational and incidental causes, has been linked with varying degrees of certainty to a range of health effects. To the non-medical or non-political mind the evidence can be confusing and many opinions are voiced with varying degrees of bias and misconception. However, it is now widely accepted that asbestos dust can be the cause of crippling and painful conditions which may ultimately hasten death. The levels of exposure which may be safe or unsafe remain to be fully quantified and therefore in terms of safety and prudence the term 'minimum practical levels' will be seen to occur in regulations and advice given for work in the field. This definition itself clearly is open to question, as will be seen later.

With present knowledge, it is universally agreed that exposure to asbestos fibres can in certain circumstances lead to three diseases:

- asbestosis
- lung cancer
- mesothelioma.

There are indications that it may also be linked with other cancers.

Evidence linking asbestos fibres with these diseases has been collected slowly for many years. Indeed the link between lung cancer and asbestos exposure was first observed in 1935 with earlier reports of deaths among asbestos workers due to scarring of the lung tissue. With the wisdom of hindsight, many cases of asbestos-related diseases may well have been overlooked or misdiagnosed in the past.

Asbestos exposure

It has been difficult to quantify the effects of asbestos exposure for a number of reasons.

Firstly, as was seen in Chapter 1, asbestos is not a unique chemical compound, but the generic term for a group of related mineral compounds of varying composition. These compounds have some useful properties in common which have resulted in their widespread use throughout the industrial world. Not the least useful of these properties is the ability to be broken down into fine fibres which are used in conjunction with other materials. This particular property is the one which, if continued by further work or abrasion, produces ultrafine fibres of microscopic size measured in microns (or micro metres). At these dimensions, the fibres are capable of inhalation and passage to the capilliaries of the lungs. Such inhaled fibres can be exhaled, removed with macrophages, remain in the lung or penetrate the wall. Those remaining in the body often give rise to asbestos conditions and subsequent medical problems.

Secondly, asbestos is used with other materials to form composites, the other components of which may modify its effects. Asbestos-related diseases generally take many years to be evidenced in the body and the biological effects are due in part to the physical configuration of the asbestos fibres.

Finally, but by no means least, the mechanism of human cancer formation, in spite of considerable and long-term research, is not fully understood.

In the past some gross levels of dust and fibre contamination were found in working atmospheres, especially in the asbestos factories. Such contamination levels would, under present legislation, be totally unacceptable for non-protected exposure. Those conditions would give rise to asbestosis, whereas the much reduced 'acceptable' levels now in force clearly give correspondingly reduced levels of risk.

The early measurements of pollution levels were far less accurate than those at present in use and even these are questioned in some quarters. The methods of counting fibres to determine pollution levels do not accurately predict the carcinogenic potential of the sample.

Asbestosis

Asbestosis was defined by the Advisory Council on Asbestos (1979) as fibrosis of the lungs caused by asbestos dusts. The symptoms of the disease are shortness of breath and coughing which can also be produced in other ways. Because the symptoms can be produced by other conditions, diagnosis of asbestosis during life must be a matter of judgement by the medical profession. Along with the shortness of breath and cough, other symptoms may be manifest such as clubbing of the fingers, lack of energy and weight loss. These may also indicate other serious lung disorders and heart disease.

The diagnosis therefore is made on the various physical signs, the results of noises in the lung, X-ray testing and pulmonary function testing accompanied by a history of substantial exposure to asbestos. Lung function tests are carried out to measure the efficiency of the lungs as part of such diagnosis. These tests include the 'vital capacity', the largest breath that can be expired after a full inhalation, and the 'forced expiratory volume' which is the percentage of the vital capacity expelled in one second. Some or all of these parameters may also be used in the diagnosis of mesothelioma or lung cancer.

Asbestosis develops slowly and even in the gross exposures of the past seldom caused death in less than 10 years. The severity of asbestosis depends both on the levels and length of time of that exposure.

The first apparent British recorded death from asbestosis was around 1900 when post mortem examination confirmed that the death of an asbestos spinner was caused by extensive lung scarring caused by the breathing of asbestos dust (asbestosis). This was reported to a government enquiry into compensation for industrial diseases in 1906. Under the present controls and resultant decreased exposure, no person with otherwise healthy lungs should die of asbestosis. However, in the presence of other diseases such as may result from smoking, minor fibrosis due to asbestos may aggravate the symptoms.

Lung cancer

The high level of lung cancer in the general population makes it difficult to attribute any one incidence of the disease to asbestos exposure, particularly if smoking is also involved.

Lung cancers due to asbestos are not distinguishable from lung cancers due to other causes and rarely occur less than 10 years after exposure. The risk of lung cancer can be reduced by reducing the exposure to asbestos.

However, the link between smoking and asbestos as giving increased risk is strong and an individual who smokes and has been exposed to asbestos can materially reduce his risk merely by stopping smoking.

Note that although there is an increased risk for those smokers who work with asbestos, lung cancers attributable in the event to asbestos occur proportionately to the same extent in non-smokers and smokers alike. It therefore follows that for asbestos-related lung cancer, smoking habits are not relevant in determining cause. This can be helpful in legal terms.

It is usually thought that the amphiboles crocidolite, amosite and tremolite, for which the fibres are straight, give greater risk than chrysotile, where the fibres are twisted and have a greater possibility of clumping. However, chrysotile frequently occurs with traces of tremolite impurity and this may be associated with the chrysotile risk.

Mesothelioma

Mesothelioma is a cancer of the lining of the chest or abdomen. Once a very rare cancer, this has at the same time as work on lung cancer been linked to exposure to asbestos. Links between tumours of the pleura (membrane covering the surface of the lung) and peritoneum (membrane covering the abdominal cavity) are very strong. Estimates that 85 per cent of all mesotheliomas are related to asbestos exposure are considered generally acceptable.

When caused by asbestos, mesotheliomas seldom occur within 15 years of first exposure but the period is variously reported from 10 to 50 years or more. The risk of mesothelioma is unaffected by smoking but varies with the type of asbestos. Again as with lung cancer, amphiboles present a higher risk than the serpentine chrysotile.

Other diseases

Asbestos can enter the body by ingestion as well as by inhalation. This can be directly by the intake of contaminated food or drink or indirectly by swallowing mucous.

There is evidence to correlate gastro-intestinal cancer with exposure to asbestos, but at a lower rate than for lung cancer. However, experiments have shown that no such cancer is produced with asbestos in animals and initial examination of the available evidence suggests that the observations are largely or wholly due to misdiagnosis of lung cancer or mesothelioma.

Other studies have linked asbestos to cancer of the larynx with somewhat lower risks than for lung cancer. Possible links to cancer of the ovaries or kidneys have been made, but the available data are too few for conclusions to be drawn about the causes.

Laboratory evidence

As well as work on medical diagnosis and links with reports of the various diseases, work has been carried out in laboratories in an effort to confirm the various hazard potentials noted from medical evidence. These latter experiments have been made under controlled conditions and, whilst not necessarily conclusive, mirror those carried out for other diseases and under similar protocols.

These laboratory tests suggest that the hazard is greatest with fibres between 5 and 100 microns in length and of less than 1.5-2.0 microns diameter. There do not appear to be sharp boundaries between hazardous and non-hazardous configurations. Short fibres of less than 1 or 2 microns in length may not be hazardous at all but there is no evidence of any minimum diameter below which fibres may not be carcinogenic. Such ultrafine fibres have diameters so small that they cannot be seen by the optical microscope currently used for control testing. They can be detected by scanning or transmission electron microscopy. However, these instruments cannot simply be used for routine control purposes.

Current regulatory standards which count fibres more than 5 microns long with aspect ratios (length to diameter) of more than 3 to 1 may, therefore, not be the most appropriate.

This testing has shown that all types of asbestos that have been used in industry will produce pulmonary fibrosis (asbestosis), lung cancer and mesothelioma in animals. It has also shown that the conditions are produced at much the same frequency when equal numbers of fibres are compared. No gastro-intestinal cancers have been produced by any of the main commercial asbestos types.

These studies show that there is a conflict in the conclusion relating to chrysotile in which the Advisory Committee on Asbestos (1979) found that chrysotile and amosite were less carcinogenic than crocidolite, but it was reported by Doll and Peto (*Effects on Health of Exposure to Asbestos* HMSO, 1985) that animal studies point to chrysotile being at least as damaging and possibly more so than crocidolite (or amosite) at equal respirable mass exposure concentrations and much more damaging for equal amounts retained in the lungs.

-However, it would be reasonable to conclude that all types of asbestos should be treated with equal caution especially where there is the risk of production of airborne fibres. This occurs particularly with asbestos removal operations for maintenance, demolition or refurbishing. Subsequent sections will detail the precautions taken in such work and the regulations and codes of practice relating to the work.

Chapter 3

THE LEGAL FRAMEWORK TO 1980

In 1906, it was reported to a government enquiry into compensation for industrial diseases that the post-mortem examination into the death of an asbestos spinner had shown that he died from extensive scarring of the lung tissue caused by asbestos dust.

In 1930, an official enquiry, the Mereweather and Price Report, confirmed that the incidence of specific diseases could be related to work with asbestos. As a direct result of this enquiry, Asbestos Regulations were introduced in 1931 which became effective in 1933.

These regulations applied to factories using asbestos as a primary manufacturing material and required them to be registered. The list covered the asbestos textile industry, producers of insulation products, brake linings and asbestos cement products. However the regulations did not cover supplementary use such as the removal and replacement of asbestos insulation and thus were deficient in their control of the material.

Although conditions had improved in certain industries, this deficiency in cover coupled with evidence that there was a continuous increase in the incidence of asbestos-related diseases resulted in the Asbestos Regulations 1969.

Prior to this, there were a number of general clauses in other statutes which could apply to the control of use of asbestos. These include:

Mines and Quarries Act 1954
Agriculture (Safety, Health and Welfare) Act 1956
Factories Act 1961
Offices, Shops and Railway Premises Act 1963
Notification of Diseases Regulations 1966
Health and Safety at Work etc. Act 1974
Asbestos (Licensing) Regulations 1983
Control of Pollution Act 1974.

Mines and Quarries Act 1954

Section 74 requires that dust given off, which by its nature or quantity is likely to be harmful to employees, must be reduced to a minimum and any accumulation removed or made safe. Section 112 places a general duty on employers to protect employees from dangerous dusts which could be inhaled. However, since asbestos is not mined or quarried in this country, these sections would have to be applied to any operation within the mine or quarry that produced asbestos dust.

Agriculture (Safety, Health and Welfare) Act 1956 and Offices, Shops and Railway Premises Act 1963

Neither of these Acts deals specifically with asbestos, but both relate to safety and health in employment and hence problems of exposure to asbestos dust could be dealt with under these Acts. Such action would be taken under the provision of 'any apparent health risk' and the general cleanliness provisions.

Factories Act 1961

Section 63 deals with airborne dust and the hygiene standards to be employed in relevant factories. The Asbestos Regulations 1969 and Notification of Diseases Regulations 1966 are both made under the Factories Act. The Asbestos Regulations 1969 covered a much wider sphere of application than those of 1931 and included both construction and demolition sites.

Asbestos Regulations 1969

The Asbestos Regulations overrode the Factories Act requirements in respect of processes capable of emitting asbestos dust.

In these, asbestos is defined as:

Crocidolite, amosite, chrysotile or fibrous anthophyllite or any mixture of these.

'Asbestos dust' is taken to mean dust containing or consisting of asbestos to such a degree as to present a health hazard to workers.

The Asbestos Regulations 1969 were applied to:

building construction, repair or demolition;
constructional engineering sites;
generating stations;
factories, and
ships in dry dock or harbour.

The requirements are that dust should be controlled to the minimum practical level to prevent danger to the health of employees. This was based on the application of threshold limit values (TLV) which later were reclassified as control limits. The TLV referred to the amount of dust in the workplace atmosphere together with the duration of the exposure.

The TLVs established under the Regulations were:

Crocidolite　　　　0.2 fibres per ml measured over a 10-minute period

Amosite, chrysotile   2 fibres per ml over a 4-hour period;
and fibrous   12 fibres per ml over a 10-minute
Anthophyllite   period.

Under today's control limits these figures seem extremely high, but the interpretation of 'minimum practical' must be seen in the context of the time.

In addition to the threshold limit values, further controls and actions were required as follows:

General – Asbestos Regulations, Parts I and VI

1   The Asbestos Regulations 1969 apply to every process involving asbestos or any article composed wholly or partly of asbestos in which asbestos dust is given off in any factory, premises or place.

2   It is the duty of every employer or contractor to comply with these Regulations in relation to himself if self-employed, and any person employed by him, any plant or materials under his control in any factory or part of a factory where he is engaged in processing materials containing asbestos. It is also the duty of every person employed to comply with the Regulations.

3   Any occupier of any factory where any processing involving asbestos material is being carried on, whether or not he is the employer as set out above, is similarly responsible under the Regulations for the provision of protective equipment and its accommodation and cleaning in relation to any person employed by him where the asbestos dust concentrations are above the acceptable level, and for the cleanliness of premises and plant.

4   The extent to which the precautions need to be taken in order to comply with the Regulations is related to the concentration of asbestos dust in the breathing zone of the operatives, together with the duration of the exposure.

5   The Chief Inspector may, in certain circumstances, by certificate in writing, issue an exemption against all or any part of the Regulations subject to his being satisfied that they are not necessary for the protection of the persons employed.

6   Where a person proposed to undertake in any factory any process involving crocidolite (blue asbestos) the local factory inspector must be given 28 days', or less by agreement, written notice.

7   No young person under eighteen years of age may be employed where the Regulations call for use of protective equipment.

Exhaust ventilation and protective equipment – Asbestos Regulations, Parts II and V

1   The Regulations require that the processing be carried on under an exhaust draught or in some other equally safe manner designed to ensure that the concentration of airborne asbestos dust entering the work place is not above the acceptable level. Where this is not practicable, approved forms of respirator and protective clothing must be provided.

2   Exhaust equipment is to be inspected once in every seven days and tested by a competent person in every 14-month period. A report on the test is to be attached to the general register and kept available for inspection for a period of 2 years.

3   Respiratory equipment and protective clothing, where necessary, shall be well maintained and cleaned, with suitable accommodation provided. No respirator is to be worn by more than one person unless it has first been thoroughly cleaned and disinfected. No person shall be employed on work where respiratory equipment is required unless he has been properly instructed in its use.

Cleanliness of premises and plant – Asbestos Regulations, Part III

1   It is a duty to keep free from asbestos waste and dust, in so far as this is practicable, all plant and machinery, exhaust and ventilation equipment, and all internal surfaces of the building. Vacuum cleaning equipment or other dustless methods, such as wetting before and during sweeping, should be used for this purpose, and where this is impracticable, personnel undertaking the cleaning and any others in the close vicinity must be provided with protective equipment.

2   Vacuum cleaning equipment provided in accordance with the Regulations must be regularly maintained and cleaned.

3   Buildings used for the first time for a scheduled process (see regulation 12 of the Asbestos Regulations 1969) for a period exceeding 8 hours per week, must satisfy these requirements:

   (a) all the interior surfaces must be smooth, impervious, and with the minimum of dust-trapping surfaces; and

   (b) a vacuum cleaning system shall form part of the permanent structure.

Storage and distribution – Asbestos Regulations, Part IV

All loose asbestos fibre in a factory, both virgin and waste materials, should be stored and distributed in suitably closed receptacles to prevent the emission of dust.

Health and Safety at Work etc. Act 1974

Apart from the Asbestos Regulations 1969 the main legislation used for the control of asbestos at work has been the Health and Safety at Work etc. Act 1974.

Even though neither the Act itself nor any of the regulations made up to 1987 has dealt specifically with asbestos, the Act has been used in its general context. This places a general requirement on employers, employees and manufacturers alike to maintain or help to maintain safe working conditions. Again the term 'reasonably practical' can be used to argue a trade off on the risks to health and the improvement or control measures taken. However, the wording can and has been used in conjunction with codes of practice and guidance notes to force employers to adopt safety standards in excess of those set out in any regulations if it can be shown that they are reasonably practical to attain.

In particular, this approach was used by the Health and Safety Executive in applying Guidance Note EH10, Asbestos – Control Limits, measurement of asbestos dust and assessment of control measures in conjunction with the Asbestos Regulations 1969 to working environments to which they would not normally apply.

The Health and Safety at Work etc. Act can apply only particular hygiene standards to work with asbestos. It is then left to the employer or manufacturer to decide how to react to meet these standards.

The obligations under the Health and Safety at Work etc. Act 1974 are prescribed under the general duties contained in sections 2, 3, 4 and 6 of the Act. Employers have a duty:

- to protect the health, safety and welfare of their employees at work, as far as is reasonably practical.
- to protect the health, safety and welfare of persons not at work (i.e. the public) so far as is reasonably practical and that any undertakings are conducted in a manner which will not put at risk the health and safety of those persons.
- to ensure that premises at which work is carried out by persons who are not employed by the owner of those premises will not put at risk the health and safety of those persons, e.g. contractors or subcontractors carrying out work at the premises. It also requires that adequate information be made available to those persons of the health risks of products on which they are required to work.
- that manufacturers, designers and suppliers ensure that substances used in the work environment are safe.

Control of Pollution Act 1974

The Control of Pollution Act 1974 is the major legislation dealing with waste disposal. The Act is relevant to the control of asbestos in a number of spheres.

First, it requires the waste disposal authority to draw up plans for waste disposal. These plans must take into account the disposal of hazardous wastes which include asbestos.

Second, it requires that waste disposal sites should be licensed to ensure that disposal is carried out without unacceptable risk to the environment, public health, safety or amenity.

Section 17, special chemical waste regulations provide for the documented control of all hazardous wastes of which asbestos is one.

Chapter 4

THE LEGAL
FRAMEWORK
POST-1980

In the period since 1980-81 the Health and Safety Commission has invoked the Health and Safety at Work etc. Act 1974 as a means of controlling work with asbestos which was not necessarily covered by the Asbestos Regulations.

In particular the code of practice for 'work with asbestos insulation and asbestos coatings' was approved by the Health and Safety Commission in 1981. This required specific procedures to be applied by contractors working with insulation and coating materials.

It was modified to take account of more stringent control limits and a fuller revision was subsequently made necessary by the introduction of new legislation which included:

Asbestos (Licensing) Regulations 1983;
Asbestos (Prohibition) Regulations 1986, and
Control of Asbestos at Work Regulations 1987.

The original approved code of practice for work with asbestos insulation and coatings was accompanied by a guidance note, but the Health and Safety Executive decided that this should be replaced by a series of guidance notes. These give a more detailed cover to the various aspects of the work and procedures. Whilst they are not statutory requirements, if they are not followed, it becomes the duty of those working with asbestos to provide proof that they have complied with relevant legislation 'by another means'.

Separate guidance notes have been issued for work with asbestos materials which are not classified as insulation or coatings.

Asbestos Licensing Regulations 1983

The Code of Practice for work with asbestos insulation and asbestos coating issued in 1981 did not stipulate that the work should be carried out by specialists. However, to conform to the code did require a specialist approach by the person carrying out the work. This specialization was reinforced by the Asbestos (Licensing) Regulations 1983 and, prior to the issue of the 1987 Control of Asbestos Regulations, made the biggest impact on the industry.

The Asbestos (Licensing) Regulations 1983 are issued under relevant sections of the Health and Safety at Work etc. Act 1974 and make it virtually impossible for non-licensed persons to carry out work with asbestos insulation or coatings.

The interpretations of the regulations widen the definition of asbestos and clearly define the differences between asbestos materials. This widening of the definitions indicates the greater knowledge which has been gained over the years since the Asbestos Regulations 1969 came into being.

The interpretations in the Asbestos (Licensing) Regulations are as follows:

'asbestos' means any of the following materials, that is to say crocidolite, amosite, chrysotile, fibrous actinolite, fibrous anthophyllite, fibrous tremolite, and any mixture containing any of these materials;

'asbestos cement' means a material which is predominantly a mixture of cement and which when in the dry state has a density greater than 1 tonne per cubic metre;

'asbestos coating' means a surface coating which contains asbestos;

'asbestos insulation' means any material containing asbestos and used for thermal, acoustic or other insulation purposes (including fire protection) except:

(*a*)   asbestos cement or asbestos insulating board or

(*b*)   any article of bitumen, plastic, resin or rubber which contains asbestos and the thermal and acoustic properties of which are incidental to its main purpose; 'asbestos insulating board' means any sheet, tile or building board consisting of a mixture of asbestos and other material which mixture when in a dry state has a density greater than 500 kilograms per cubic metre; 'work with asbestos insulation or asbestos coating' means work in which asbestos insulation and asbestos coating is removed, replaced or disturbed and includes such work in a supervisory or ancillary capacity.

Work with asbestos insulation or asbestos coating may be carried out by non-licensed persons, provided that no one person spends more than a total of one hour on such work in any period of seven days and that the total time spent by all persons on that work does not exceed two hours. Additionally for any such small amount of work, formal notice is required to the enforcing authority at least 28 days prior to commencement (or such shorter period as that authority may allow).

Therefore, with the exception of the stringent time-related aspect of work by unlicensed persons, the general requirements of the licensing regulations will still apply.

The only other area of work with asbestos and asbestos coatings for which a licence is not required is that which consists of air monitoring or collecting of samples for the purposes of identification. This will be dealt with later.

The Health and Safety Executive may grant a licence for work with asbestos insulation or asbestos coating if appropriate to any person who applies for such a licence in the correct manner. It may apply specific conditions to such a licence when issued and may vary or omit or add to existing conditions. 'Asbestos licences' may be revoked for contravention of restrictions or regulations or failure to discharge a duty relating to the work under the Health and Safety at Work etc. Act. The regulations also require the employer to ensure that his employees who work with asbestos insulation or asbestos coatings are kept under medical surveillance. Medical examinations should be carried out at least every two years by an employment medical adviser or by a doctor appointed to carry out such medical examinations by the Health and Safety Executive. The medical certificate or a copy of it must be retained for at least 4 years from the date of the medical examination.

The regulations also apply to self-employed persons carrying out such work.

The regulations apply to work outside Great Britain when the Health and Safety at Work etc. Act 1974 (Application Outside Great Britain) Order 1977 (SI 1977 No. 1232) applies.

In the event of any revocation of the licence, the Health and Safety at Work etc. Act 1974 provides for the licence holder to appeal against the decision.

The Asbestos (Prohibitions) Regulations 1985

These regulations came into force in January 1986, and were issued under relevant clauses of the Health and Safety at Work etc. Act 1974.

The interpretations are as for the Asbestos (Licensing) Regulations but with the following additions:

> 'asbestos insulation – the exceptions are extended to include: film foil, resin or rubber-coated asbestos textiles primarily used for fire protection and asbestos spraying is added;
>
> 'asbestos spraying' means the application by spraying of any material containing asbestos to form a surface coating, but does not include the application by spraying of any bituminous composition containing less than 10 per cent, by weight of asbestos to motor vehicles for the purpose of undersealing.

The prohibitions apply in all circumstances except where specific exemption is given or where the materials are imported solely for the purposes of assessment or evaluation.

The regulations specifically prohibit the supply or use of any product containing crocidolite or amosite for any new work except for work in disposal of the product.

They further prohibit any asbestos spraying or the installation of asbestos insulation.

The regulations are extended outside Great Britain by the same procedure as in the Asbestos (Licensing) Regulations 1983.

Control of Asbestos at Work Regulations 1987

The Control of Asbestos at Work Regulations are made under relevant sections of the Health and Safety at Work etc. Act 1974. In the build-up to these regulations the Health and Safety Commission has taken into account provision of two European Community directives on asbestos, 83/477/EEC and 83/478/EEC, which were adopted in September 1983. It has also taken into account recommendations made by the Advisory Committee on Asbestos relating to the work place and which are not covered by the existing or proposed legislation.

The new regulations are intended to replace the existing Asbestos Regulations 1969 which are not considered suitable for implementation of the Asbestos Worker Protection Directive 83/477/EEC. Equally whilst the Health and Safety at Work etc. Act 1974 covers all activities related to asbestos, the requirements are so general that the obligations both on employers or employees are not always clearly understood.

The Control of Asbestos Regulations therefore have been prepared together with a code of practice which gives guidance on the requirements of the regulations to ensure that the control of asbestos at work, in all aspects, is consistent with advances made since 1969 and to allow for further advance in the future under one set of regulations.

The regulations apply to all work with asbestos from which exposure of persons to asbestos may arise. This is taken to include as well as the manufacture processing, all work in installation, maintenance or removal of asbestos products, the handling, storage, distribution and disposal etc. of asbestos-containing materials.

The regulations have specific requirements where in the past there has been an implied requirement. This imposes an additional burden on all persons involved in work with asbestos.

There is a legal requirement to carry out an assessment before starting work which may involve exposure to asbestos. Such assessment must identify the nature and degree of exposure to allow determination of the precautions needed to ensure compliance with other regulations.

Employers are required to give specific information to their employees and persons affected by their work on asbestos.

Control measures are required by the use of correct procedures to limit exposure and to minimize the spread of contamination. This applies whether or not personal protective equipment is in use and includes the provision of basic hygiene measures.

The requirement for medical surveillance is now included for all work with asbestos where there is a risk of exposure to asbestos dust.

The control limits were set in August 1984 but it is important to note that there remains an over-riding duty to reduce exposure to the lowest reasonably practical level. In addition to the control limits the regulations bring into force the use of action levels. This procedure sets levels below the control limit at which additional precautions are taken but also ensures that they are not taken except where necessary.

Whilst in many instances air monitoring has been carried out, the regulations, for the first time, introduce a specific requirement to assess compliance with the control limit and the duty to minimize exposure and, where appropriate, for the purposes of assessment.

Regulation 15 requires employers to ensure that laboratories which they use for sample analysis have the necessary facilities, expertise and quality control procedures to provide accurate results. This can be secured by laboratories accredited by NATLAS for airborne asbestos measurement by methods in HSE guidance. NATLAS is the National Testing Laboratory Accreditation Scheme. It is now part of the UK's National Measurement Accreditation Scheme (NAMAS) and laboratories can refer to either NATLAS or NAMAS accreditation. If a non-accredited laboratory is used, employers should satisfy themselves that the laboratory meets the requirements as set out above. This, in effect, means that laboratories not accredited by NATLAS should have facilities, expertise and quality control procedures at least as good as those required to achieve accreditation. The requirements are discussed later.

Code of practice

In conjunction with the Control of Asbestos Regulations, the Health and Safety Commission has issued a revised code of practice for work with asbestos insulation, asbestos coatings and asbestos insulating board. This takes full account of all the improvements and revised legislation referred to above.

The Health and Safety Executive has in the past issued a series of guidance notes relating to asbestos. The series is being updated and extended to take account of recent new legislation. These guidance notes give detailed advice on procedures which will ensure compliance with the code of practice and the Control of Asbestos at Work Regulations.

The main points in the code of practice are summarized below.

Duties

Under the regulations the employer has a duty to minimize the exposure of his employees to asbestos. He will similarly have a like duty to protect other persons who are not in his employ but may be affected by his work on asbestos. This is particularly so when asbestos coatings or insulation are being removed, since the work is often carried out by contractors on other occupiers' premises.

Assessment

Work with asbestos insulation, asbestos coatings and asbestos insulating board will effectively always lead to exposures above the action level and generally the control limit.

The assessment required by the regulations therefore must be in writing and must be specific for the actual job to be performed.

The practice of preparing method statements is already followed by many contractors, but too frequently the method statement is standardized. The revised procedures called for in the code of practice require specific method statements for specific jobs.

Control measures

Previous versions of the code of practice required only that asbestos dust should be contained within the work area. The present version requires that dust release within the enclosure should be kept to the minimum reasonably practical level. This clearly emphasizes that work on asbestos should be carried out in an area separated from its surroundings and also that the methods of work should be such as to limit release within that enclosed area.

One area which may give difficulty, particularly in demolition, is the fact that the code of practice 'prefers' an enclosure as the method of containment. The provision for safe distance segregation is not included. This clearly can cause problems, for example when extended runs of insulated pipework require to be delagged for repair or replacement of the insulation in exposed trenches.

Designated areas

When working with insulation or coating it should normally be assumed that exposures in the enclosure and the 'dirty end' of the decontamination facility will be liable to exceed the control limit. By the same reasoning, where employees working with asbestos are required to transit from the work area to decontamination facilities they are by definition not fully decontaminated. Thus it becomes essential to continue the wearing of respiratory protection equipment until undressed in the hygienic facilities proper.

Air monitoring

The code of practice gives a number of applications of air monitoring. Although this may be limited by the short duration of some activities it is accepted that within enclosures respirators will be worn as a matter of course.

However, on longer-term activities, air monitoring provides a very good measure of control and ensures compliance with the procedures. Further it can give assurance to persons who may be affected by the work. There is therefore likely to be an increased awareness of the need and advantages of air monitoring around and in the work areas.

Clearance testing in areas when asbestos insulation or coatings have been worked requires a clearance level of 0.010 fibres per millilitre of air or less.

The code recommends that laboratories carrying out air monitoring work in association with work on asbestos insulation or asbestos coating should be accredited by NATLAS. This is intended to provide a standardization of procedures for the air monitoring work and a common standard amongst analysts.

Medical surveillance

Medical surveillance is required for all employees working with asbestos. However, the occupation health records for exposure during asbestos removal are likely to be difficult to maintain since the work generally involves a number of short or relatively short-term projects.

The various aspects of these latest regulations are examined in relation to the specific aspects in subsequent chapters. Typical codes of practice as would be prepared by persons working within the spheres covered by the regulations and code of practice are included as appendices. If such are prepared by employers they should be made available to the staff and also may be required by clients prior to work on their sites.

Chapter 5

LOCATION,
TREATMENT
AND REMOVAL

Assessment

It will have been noted in the opening chapter that asbestos products have been widely used throughout industry and construction – in insulation of pipework and vessels, structural materials, fire protection, acoustic insulation and decorative finishes.

The various regulations require that the employer shall not carry out any work which is liable to expose any of his employees (or persons not his employees) to asbestos, unless he has made an adequate assessment of that exposure.

Clearly in the widest interpretation of this duty, the employer must know the location and condition of asbestos materials on his premises. Many employers/occupiers already have this information but the implication is clear, that those who do not should obtain it. This will require a survey of the premises or factory with a documentation procedure which is maintained as a register of asbestos.

The information becomes particularly relevant when repairs or maintenance are required to plant and machinery or the building fabric. The contractor or in-house maintenance staff can then be advised of the asbestos situation.

The survey should include location, material type and use, asbestos content and type, condition and action necessary. Any work carried out should also be recorded so as to update the assessment.

Procedures should also be established to include any materials which are subsequently found after the initial survey. All known asbestos materials should be clearly marked with the approved asbestos label.

Asbestos occurs in a wide range of situations and materials as illustrated in Table 5.1.

Table 5.1

Asbestos products

Type	Composition	Typical locations
Coatings		
Spray coatings (insulation)	Minimum 55 per cent asbestos by weight in combination with cement and inert fillers. Asbestos may be present as crocidolite, amosite or chrysotile in any combination. Other asbestos minerals may be present but unlikely.	Fire protection on ceilings, columns or structural steel. Acoustic insulation in large duct work.
Surface coatings (decorative)	Variable content of short chrysotile fibres, cement, paint pigments.	Decorative finishes to ceilings or walls.
Sectional high-fibre content	80-90 per cent asbestos bound with sodium silicate binder. May be in block form or preformed sections for pipework. Generally long fibre amosite but can be chrysotile or crocidolite.	Pipework Vessels Boilers Firebreaks
Calcium silicate	15-30 per cent chrysotile with calcium silicate. Note that recent formulations contain glass fibre and can be mistakenly 'identified' if not correctly sampled and analysed.	Pipework Vessels Boilers
Magnesium	15 per cent amosite, chrysotile with basic magnesium carbonate	Boilers Vessels Pipework

Type	Composition	Typical locations
'Hard set' Many varied types	10-55 per cent asbestos in mixture with amosite, chrysotile and crocidolite in a mixture with chalk, cement or other fillers. Usually smooth polished surfaces as initially put in place. May also contain non-asbestos fibres such as jute, horsehair, straw, synthetic organic fibres or glass fibre.	Pipework Vessels Boilers
Asbestos boards and sheets		
Asbestos insulating board for insulating or fire proofing	15-25 per cent asbestos, generally amosite but may include chrysotile or amosite	Ceiling panels, Stud work partitioning Linings Fireproofing Firebreaks in ductwork
Mill boards	45-95 per cent asbestos, generally chrysotile	Ceiling panels Partitioning Fireproofing Firebreaks
Asbestos cement	10-15 per cent asbestos, mainly chrysotile but may include amosite and if pre-1960 also crocidolite	Corrugated sheets, flat sheets as roofing, cladding, ceiling panels, partitioning, drainage pipes, gutterings, flues, firebreaks.
Other products		
Asbestos textiles	Chrysotile generally up to 98 per cent, rarely crocidolite	Fire blankets, curtains, woven lagging or pillows etc., switchgear.
Rope	Up to 99 per cent asbestos of any type, generally chrysotile	Plugging or filling for doors, lagging exhaust systems etc.

Type	Composition	Typical locations
Friction products	25-70 per cent, generally chrysotile bound with phenolic resin and inert fillers	Brake pads Clutch pads
Reinforced plastics	20-50 per cent asbestos of any type or mixture in thermoplastic or thermosetting resin	Moulded or sheet products generally with electrical equipment
Packings, jointings, sealants, roofing felts	These materials may contain asbestos of any type as well as other fillers in a variety of binders	Gaskets, sealants for oven doors, roof coverings etc.

Based on the table and identification analysis carried out by others, the data obtained from the recovery should be incorporated into the asbestos register for the site or building.

A typical assessment/record form for inclusion in the register is shown in Table 5.2.

Table 5.2

Example of assessment/record form

Asbestos Register	Sheet No

Premises
Date of entry to register
Location of asbestos material   Plant Room No. 123
Specific duty/use of asbestos   Insulation of pipework
and
          Boilers
          Ceiling tiles
          Fire breaks
          Electrical equipment

Type of asbestos:
  Crocidolite   Insulation
  Amosite   Insulation, ceiling tiles
  Chrysotile   Insulation, firebreaks, electrical

  Other   None

Condition of asbestos
1 Some insulation damaged, remainder
   good condition and painted.
2 Ceiling tiles – not painted, some cracked.
3 Firebreaks not painted and rough edges.
4 Electrical equipment has woven fabric in
   fuse clips.

Assessment of exposure risk
1 Work in areas where insulation is damaged could cause
   fibre release.
   Work on pipework will require asbestos to be removed.
2 Ceiling tiles – low risk.
3 Fire breaks – low risk.
4 Electrical equipment – low risk.

Actions
A Immediate:
   Carry out air tests to establish risk.
   Spray seal damaged areas, ceiling and fire breaks.
   Label all asbestos products.
   Place warning signs at entrance to area.
   Establish permit to work procedure.

B Planned work:
   Contractors/employees to be advised of asbestos content.
   Longer-term remove and replace with non-asbestos
      products.

In this manner the potential pitfalls of unauthorized working on asbestos materials will be minimized and the resultant difficulties of cessation of sometimes essential repairs will be overcome at the planning stage.

Such surveys require an extensive knowledge of the premises since the asbestos will not always be evident. Specialist contractors or surveyors can be employed to carry out the surveys and they will have the experience of knowing where to probe.

Sampling

To complete the assessment form as shown in Table 5.2 it will be necessary to obtain samples of the materials suspected to contain asbestos. They may not all be asbestos but sampling should be representative.

Recommendations for sampling of asbestos materials or those suspected to be asbestos are given in the following publications:

Asbestos Control Limits, measurement of airborne dust concentration and the assessment of control measures, Guidance Note EH10, Health and Safety Executive;

Recommendations for the Sampling and Identification of Asbestos in Asbestos Products, Technical Note No. 3, Asbestosis Research Council.

Sampling of bulk material is necessary, first, to determine the presence of asbestos and, second, to identify the type of asbestos – particularly crocidolite or amosite.

If, however, employers find it more convenient to treat the material as though it were crocidolite or amosite and to provide precautions appropriate for these types of asbestos, the sampling and analysis need not be undertaken other than to ensure that the bulk material is or is not asbestos.

Note that 28 days' notice is required of work on all materials containing crocidolite, although the inspectors may accept shorter periods of notice in some circumstances. Similar notice will be required for all work on asbestos insulation, asbestos coatings or asbestos insulating board in accordance with the Asbestos (Licensing) Regulations 1983 and Control of Work with Asbestos Regulations 1987.

These recommendations apply specifically to the sampling of bulk materials containing, or suspected to contain, asbestos, when samples are to be submitted for identification of their asbestos content.

Sampling should be undertaken by a trained and competent person. Laboratories can only analyse the samples they receive and any sampling which is not truly representative cannot produce valid results. Hence, the person who takes the sample holds as much responsibility as the person who analyses it. This point has been frequently overlooked in the past and can lead to unnecessary dispute.

In view of the variability of some installations, it is most important that samples taken should be entirely representative

These two pictures show damaged insulation on tank and pipework with debris on the floor.

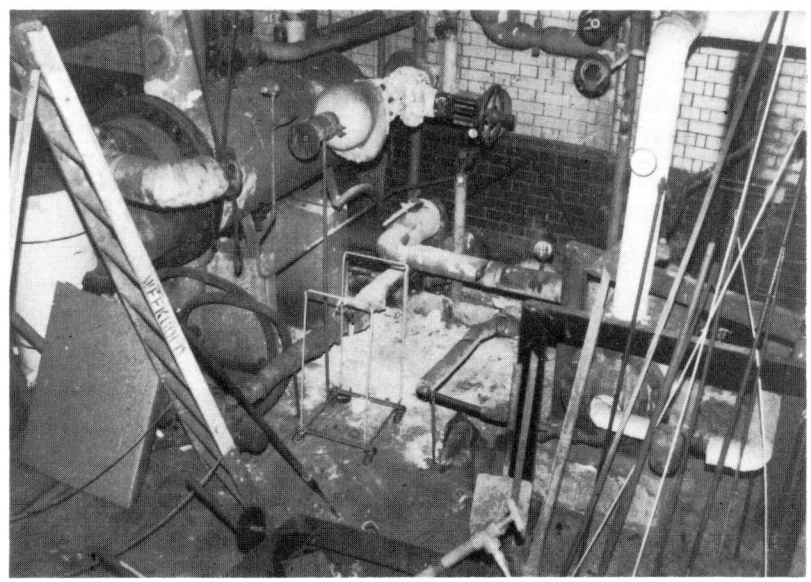

Pipe in roof space with damaged bend and debris on the floor.

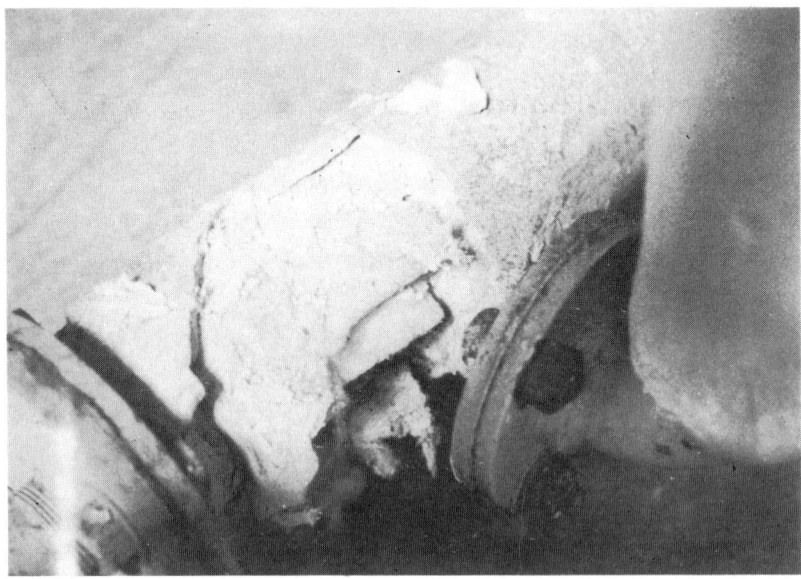

Severely damaged pipe insulation.

Roof space with debris and unused asbestos.

Non-typical example of amosite used as loose fill.

These two pictures are examples of boiler and pipe work insulation encapsulated and in good condition.

of the site situation. Therefore, several sites should be selected where the visible appearance of the material is representative of the area under review.

Where samples are taken of insulation, the sample should be to the full depth of the insulation from its outer surface to the base of the structure. It is generally recommended that a coring tool be used of around 1-inch diameter. On other materials which are much more uniform samples should be taken at a point where the least damage will be made, i.e. at the corner edge of sheets.

When sampling insulation on pipework it is important to have a knowledge of the properties of the various types of asbestos as this will assist in deciding on representative sampling. For example, crocidolite is more flexible and more easily moulded than amosite and on older installations is most likely to be found on bends and Ts in the system. It is not uncommon to find a mixture of crocidolite, amosite and chrysotile used in different sections of an installation either separately or together.

Each sample of bulk material taken should be placed in a separate sealed container to avoid cross-contamination. The container must be clearly labelled to identify the source of the sample for later reference to the assessment record. It is also important that personal hygiene is maintained during and after sampling.

On completion of the sampling all holes or cuts must be covered or filled to prevent release of asbestos fibres. No matter how carefully samples are taken, there is a risk that the action will give rise to a quantity of respirable dust. Persons taking samples, therefore, must be fully aware of the environmental hazards involved and take essential precautions for their own protection and for others in the vicinity. Areas can be wetted prior to sampling and the sample then dried before analysis in the laboratory.

Personal protective equipment should be worn under most circumstances and particularly if the area to be sampled has asbestos materials in a poor or damaged state.

A licence is not required when taking samples of asbestos materials.

Once the assessment and sampling is completed it will be possible to decide on the action to be taken. Clearly cost will be an important factor but this is not acceptable as a reason for doing nothing.

Options

Having obtained details of the location, type and condition of asbestos present, an informed judgement may be made, based on the data provided in the survey/asbestos register. This should take account of all the evidence collected and the degree of risk presented to employees or contractors who may be required to work in the area or on the materials in question.

A number of options are open which include short-term, long-term or indefinite actions:

- Do nothing
- Set up warning signs and permit to works
- Treatment to minimize risk
- Removal and replacement.

Do nothing – if the asbestos is in good condition, painted or otherwise encapsulated, the location is such that it presents little or no risk to personnel and there is little risk of damage; AND the material or area is clearly identified as having an asbestos content with a permit to work requirement.

Minimal action – if the asbestos is in good condition, painted or otherwise encapsulated, the location is such that it presents little or no risk to personnel and there is little risk of damage, BUT the material or area is not clearly identified. Post warning labels and signs and establish a permit to work requirement.

Treatment

Where the material is not in good condition but is in locations where it is not likely to be disturbed or damaged, it is reasonable to consider remedial treatment on any previously damaged or non-protected sections.

However, an immediate action should be to post warning notices to prevent unauthorized entry and to establish a permit to enter/permit to work requirement until satisfactory conditions prevail. Such conditions can be obtained either by treatment or removal of the offending materials. In either case, this will be followed by demonstration, using clearance inspection and airtesting, that the area is of sufficiently low risk that unrestricted general access may again be allowed.

When treatment of the asbestos is carried out, the warning signs and permit to work requirement should be left in place.

Treatment of asbestos by encapsulation is reasonable where the material is likely to remain undisturbed or where it is unlikely that it will require to be worked on or where regular access is required, but full removal is not practical immediately.

Remedial treatment will vary according to the situation and use of asbestos material.

Asbestos sheeting and board

These are usually a mixture of asbestos and cement and may be used internally as partitioning, ceiling tiles or trunking. The widest use is for external roofing and cladding of buildings.

Internal asbestos sheeting can be protected by a good alkali-resistant paint, if necessary, after taping or filling any cracks. In many instances they will be found covered with wallpaper or other decorative finishes.

Externally, asbestos cement sheets are generally left unpainted; however, where they are painted there will be a need for repainting on a routine basis.

If repainting is carried out while the existing paint film is still in good condition then standard painting practice should be followed. If the existing coating is showing signs of failure or has reached an advanced stage of weathering the entire film may require to be removed. When large areas are involved, and in cases where the old decoration is powdery, care should be taken to limit the evolution of dust which may contain asbestos. In these circumstances, wet methods should be used and the workers should take reasonable precautions in terms of personal protective equipment and personal hygiene.

Where external sheeting has weathered and/or become encrusted by moss, extreme care should be taken if repairs or maintenance are considered. Moss should not be scraped off dry but should be treated with moss killer and washed off.

On completion of remedial works, labelling and permit to work procedures should be maintained.

Insulation

Remedial treatment for damaged insulation should be carried out by experienced personnel working in accordance with the relevant regulations.

The process of encapsulation can provide totally adequate protection for general access once complete. In the encapsulation treatment the damaged section or all of the insulation will be covered with a coat of non-porous paint or a sealant generally supported by a layer of hessian. The combination provides a hard finished surface which is impermeable to asbestos fibres and will resist reasonable knocks.

The work should be carried out under controlled conditions and should be completed by a decontamination of the area and the standard clearance testing procedures as dealt with in Chapter 8. All encapsulated materials should be carefully labelled to show the presence of asbestos beneath and the requirement for permit to work if this should become necessary. If correctly carried out, encapsulation will provide low-risk working in the area after completion and at a cost somewhat less than that for removal without the need for replacement.

Removal

Whilst removal is a major operation in most instances, it is frequently the most cost effective long-term procedure. Provided that a philosophy of 'some out, all out' is adopted the area can then be declared essentially free from asbestos and all restrictions or permits relative to asbestos can be withdrawn.

It must be appreciated that removal of asbestos can be a time-consuming operation. The removal work itself forms, in most standard-sized projects, a relatively small part of the entire procedure.

The contractor must first notify the authorities, by law 28 days prior to commencement of work. The authorities may agree a shorter time following notification if they know the contractor and are happy with his general performance. It can, however, be very difficult when, as so often happens, the order is placed for work to start 'immediately'.

Further, to set up the enclosure and decontamination facilities will frequently take a similar period to the actual removal work itself.

Finally, the inspection and clearance procedures can become protracted unless a first-class decontamination of the area occurs.

Asbestos removal carried out correctly takes time and preparation. To rush the work is to court problems for completion and the adage 'more haste, less speed' is one of the most applicable to this work.

Figure 5.1 shows the correct procedure to take for the location, treatment and removal of asbestos from the workplace.

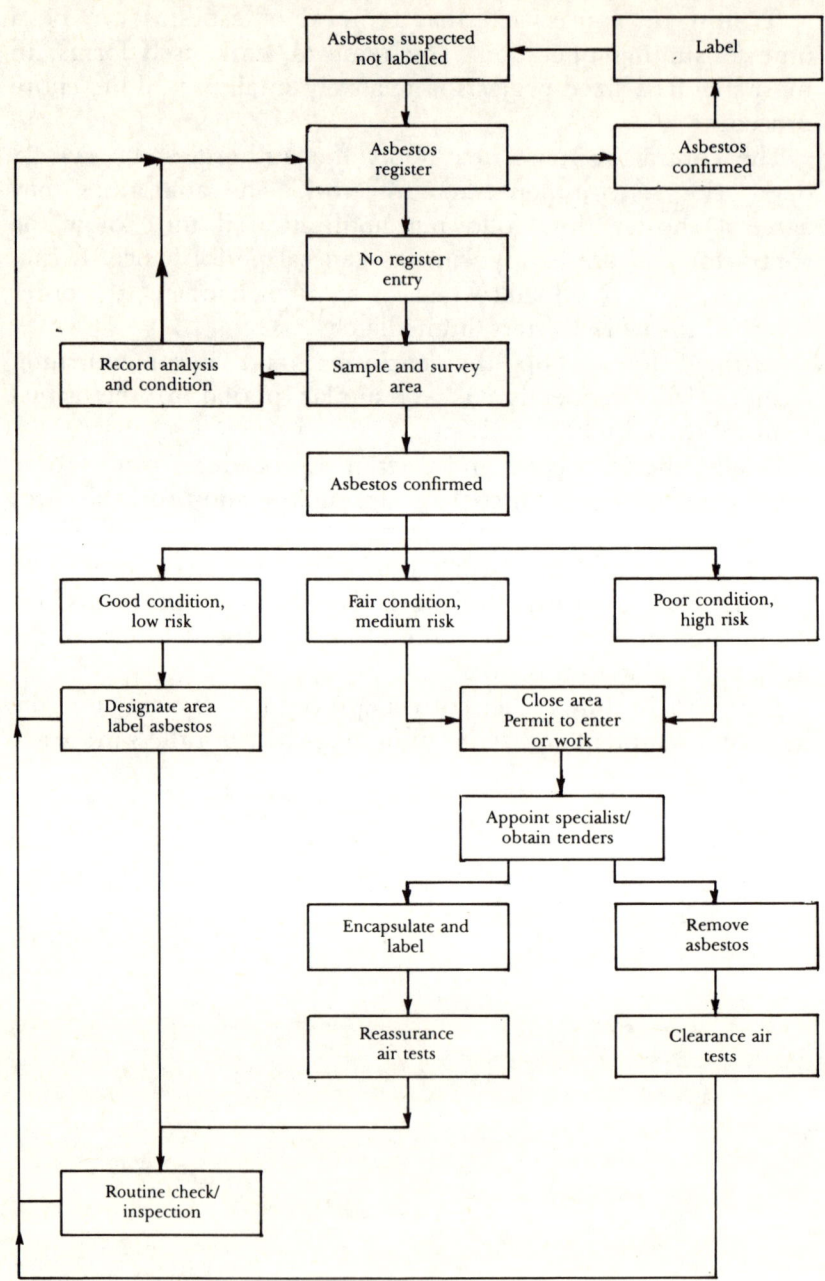

Figure 5.1   *Asbestos checklist*

Chapter 6

REMOVAL
PROCEDURES

The procedures applicable to asbestos removal are in relation to the definitions provided in the Asbestos (Licensing) Regulations 1983 which define asbestos-containing materials as:

asbestos insulation and coatings;
asbestos insulation board and
asbestos cement.

All work with asbestos insulation and coatings, i.e. those materials having a density of less than 500kg/cubic metre when dry, must be carried out in accordance with the Approved Code of Practice.

All work with asbestos insulation board, i.e. materials having a density between 500kg/cubic metre and 1 tonne/cubic metre when dry, must be carried out in accordance with Guidance Note EH37 issued by the Health and Safety Executive.

All work with asbestos cement, i.e. materials having a density of greater than 1 tonne/cubic metre when dry, must be carried out in accordance with Guidance Note EH36 issued by the Health and Safety Executive.

Over-riding all of these is the requirement to prevent or minimize, so far as is reasonably practical, the exposure of employees to asbestos as well as the duty to protect persons who are not employees.

Asbestos insulation and coatings

Asbestos insulation takes a number of forms and will be found in general on pipework or vessels associated with heating systems.

Asbestos coatings in this context generally refer to sprayed or 'limpet' asbestos although in the past a number of decorative coatings have included asbestos in their formulation to give the 'lumpy' effect.

Insulation may be present in hard setting formulations where the asbestos fibres are bound together with lime plaster and on larger pipes or vessels may also include wire mesh or expanded metal. Such materials generally contain around 50 per cent of asbestos fibre which may be present as crocidolite, amosite, chrysotile or, infrequently, the other minor fibrous minerals.

Various other combinations are encountered including preformed sections, generally of amosite containing around 80 per cent fibre. Occasionally such sectional material will be found comprising crocidolite as the fibre content.

On boilers and large installations, mats of insulation will be held in place by expanded metal or wire mesh, and are frequently sandwiched between metal sheets. Sprayed coatings will contain 80 per cent or more of asbestos and are generally of amosite or chrysotile, although occasionally a crocidolite – blue coating will be encountered. These may vary from one-half to two inches thick and are used for acoustic insulation and/or fire checks. The material is sprayed on to concrete or steel members of the building.

Removal options

Three basic procedures are available for removal of the products described above. Of these, only two are in general use for the reasons which will become evident. Essentially, however, whichever method is used, the removal requires heavy manual work to separate the asbestos from its metal or other support and to clean up the debris and package for disposal.

The three methods of insulation and coating removal are:

- dry stripping
- wet stripping
- high-pressure jetting.

Dry stripping of asbestos insulation or coatings

In this procedure which has customarily been used in smaller installations, the asbestos material is broken off its supporting metal in the dry state. Dependent on preference the workers use hatchets, hammers or other such implements to knock the material away and to the floor from where it is shovelled into bags for disposal. On completion of the rough strip, the metal work is cleaned using scrapers, wire brushes or other scouring tools, until the surfaces are clean.

Clearly these procedures will create high levels of dust and therefore they require stringent precautions to ensure that the dust is not allowed exit from the working area.

Prior to the introduction of the approved code of practice in 1981 most of the dry stripping was carried out in a dust fog which contained asbestos fibre levels of at least 100 fibres/millilitre of air.

The code of practice introduced a requirement for working under 'negative pressure' for asbestos removal. This also provided an air extract from the work zone which took with it dust contained in the work area – the air being extracted through a rough filter which protected a high efficiency particle arrestor (HEPA) filter to prevent loss of asbestos fibres to atmosphere. The process reduced the dust levels in the work area and fibre levels of 25 fibres/millilitre of air filtered appear typical if the system is set up correctly. The negative pressure air extract will also provide around ten air changes per hour.

The requirement for lowest exposure which is reasonably practical may well mean that more thought must be given to the system to reduce the levels further.

Other options for reduction of exposure level must include control of emission at source, either by local work zones in the main enclosure or by the use of such equipment as the Asbebag.

There are many instances where the dry stripping method is the only option due to the presence of electrical equipment or elevated temperatures. The use of water in quantity would exacerbate the temperature problems, leading to the additional hazards of heat stress.

Correct application of air extract can be of considerable assistance in areas where heated equipment must remain in use during removal operations. If the job is set up and planned to remove asbestos insulation with cold air passing from behind the workers towards the heated sections and thence from the enclosure, the problems of heat will be reduced. Increased air flows above the norm, or the use of local cooling must be considered. However, it is most important that the employer and the client where contractors are involved appreciate the need to work at reasonable temperatures with every effort being made to turn off all possible heating within the working enclosure.

On completion of the asbestos removal, the entire area must be scrupulously cleaned using vacuum cleaners to ensure that no residual asbestos materials are left in the enclosure. Where possible it is also advantageous to wipe all surfaces with a wet sponge to assist this cleaning. Once the work is completed it will be inspected and air tests carried out to ensure compliance with the recommended clearance conditions. This final stage should be carried out by an analyst independent of the contractor and who is approved for such work under the regulations.

Wet stripping

This procedure can be used on any work where there is no danger from live electrical equipment. It has advantages in that dust emissions are much reduced, but has disadvantages unless good housekeeping is maintained during the work. Too much water will lead to mud on the floor and the subsequent cleaning operation will become laborious and extended. Any water dicharged from the work areas must be filtered to prevent loss of asbestos to the sewers. Prior to clearance air testing, the area must be thoroughly dried out to ensure that no asbestos fibres can become airborne at a later date.

Wetting procedures depend upon the size of the job but the general approach is to allow the insulation to soak with water by syphoning or pumping into the insulation for a period of 8 to 24 hours dependent on the amount of insulation to be wetted. Ensure that excess water can run out of the insulation, e.g. by making holes at the lower edges. Also, ensure that the water does not wash the insulation off its metal surfaces. In most cases it is advantageous to protect the floor with polythene sheeting which can be lifted prior to the final inspections. On large installations, such as generating stations, this may not be practical. However, local coverings around the immediate work zone must be considered worthwhile.

The main requirement for control in these circumstances is the amount of water to be used. Too little will leave a semi-dry insulation to be worked on, too much will produce a slurry. The removal workers will be subject to wet/cold working conditions and due allowance must be made for this in the clothing, equipment and welfare facilities provided.

A number of aids to wet stripping are available, to assist in the wetting out of the material but that most used, if any, is a common detergent.

Filtration of any waste water can be provided by purpose-made filters, but experience has shown that filters prepared with manmade mineral fibre blocks to a depth of 250mm are adequate for the purpose.

Wet stripping on small installations can be carried out by wetting the insulation immediately prior to removal, but this tends to lead to 'flooding' of the work. However, the Asbebag system if properly used will contain both the water and waste asbestos.

On large installations, it is necessary to maintain control of water use, control of asbestos work zones and to limit the spread of wetted material by movement from the work area without initial hygiene procedures. The system may therefore be better described as controlled wet stripping in these circumstances.

High-pressure jetting

The use of water jets is a highly specialized technique and is therefore not widely employed. Water is jetted at approximately 140 bar (2000 psig). At this pressure the jet will cut through clothing and flesh, and therefore should be operated only by specially trained personnel.

The main use has been for removal of asbestos from areas where access is difficult. However, in the proper hands and under proper control it can be used in conjunction with the controlled wet-stripping procedure. In these circumstances, the initial wetting out can be accelerated, the rough strip carried out as normal and then the final clean completed using the high-pressure jets.

This procedure gives a much improved removal efficiency. However, it cannot be stressed too highly that incorrect use of high pressure can lead to serious injury as well as to asbestos being splashed around the area which will then require further cleaning.

Assessment of procedure to be used

Based on the descriptions above, the planned work on asbestos must consider the pros and cons of each procedure.

Dry stripping will require an extremely well-made enclosure working under negative pressure. It can be used where electrical equipment cannot be isolated or where water is liable to damage electrical equipment. If it is not possible to turn the heat off equipment to be stripped, then clearly the use of water will lead to high humidities which would only exacerbate the potential heat stress problems for the workers. Dry stripping with negative pressure air extract will lead to airborne fibre levels within the enclosure of 25 or more fibres per millilitre.

Controlled wet stripping can be used where it is not reasonably practical to prepare a total enclosure. Provided that electrical equipment can be isolated or adequate precautions implemented the procedure will much reduce the airborn fibre levels within the enclosure. Experience has shown that these can be maintained at or below the control limits of 0.2 fibres per millilitre throughout extended projects. Additional care is required to prevent the build-up of slurry or loss of this slurry from the enclosure without filtration. Personal protective equipment and clothing should take account of the wet conditions. However, with the emphasis on 'lowest exposure reasonably practical' it is felt that the wet system may well gain greater favour in the future.

High-pressure jetting should not be considered as a routine procedure, except possibly on major projects where the controls can be maintained within the working enclosure.

On small projects, the use of procedures which control asbestos at source may well be considered. However, air monitoring around work should also be included on a reassurance basis.

Since much asbestos removal is involved with demolition, the option of removal of the pipework or smaller vessels with the insulation in situ has many advantages. In this case, the pipework or vessel is wrapped in polythene, labelled and then cut out as necessary for removal. It is most important, when flame cutting of pipes is carried out within relatively small enclosures, to ensure adequate ventilation to prevent the build-up of and high exposures to combustion products such as carbon dioxide, carbon monoxide, oxides of nitrogen and metal oxide fume. The practice of using angle grinders also has its potential risks unless electrically driven machines are used. The system provides rapid clearance of an area, without the time element involved in carrying out a full stripping procedure. Correctly applied and with allowance for scrap this system is economic at all pipe sizes up to six to eight inches diameter. Minor asbestos removal may be necessary to allow cutting out, but this can be carried out by skilled personnel with little or no fibre release. Nevertheless this does not permit the use of the procedure without all regulatory controls.

Chapter 7

REMOVAL ADMINISTRATION AND CONTROL

Asbestos is an emotive subject and nowhere more so than at the removal stage. It is therefore imperative that the precautions and procedures as set out in the various codes of practice and guidance notes are followed correctly. Further, when the work is likely to involve the public it is necessary that they are demonstrated to be so. The onus for such demonstration falls as much on those who plan the work as on those who carry it out. The following procedures have been found generally to meet these criteria.

Project planning

We have mentioned previously the need to have knowledge of the location, type and condition of asbestos. Unfortunately all too often this information is not available when refurbishment or demolition is programmed. If asbestos is not found until the work starts, it must then be removed before general work can continue. This creates frustration and delay.

We therefore propose the following project sequence for all work which may involve asbestos. It has been found by experience to alleviate many of the problems which might otherwise be encountered.

1 Assessment – Survey the area, take representative samples for analysis and identification. Report in detail to the client/occupier. Define levels of risk.

2 Specification of work – Prepare documentation setting out clearly the requirements for contractors to carry out the work and including as necessary preferred methods of work and arrangements to be made to inform those affected by the work.

3 Pre-contract meeting – This meeting will be held before work starts and should be attended by the contractor, the Architect/Engineer and client representatives, both management and staff. In this way, those involved will be advised and can raise their queries before work starts. It will save problems later.

4 Permit to set up site – The contractor should be issued with a permit to set up site which requires the presentation of all relevant data. This permit should be posted prominently near the work site so that others are made aware of the control.

5 Inspection of enclosure and permit to work – Once the contractor has set up site, which includes the necessary working enclosure or enclosures, this will be inspected and generally smoke tested to demonstrate its integrity. Such inspection and smoke testing should be witnessed by the Architect/Engineer, analyst and representatives of the client. When all are satisfied a permit to work should be issued and again posted prominently near the work site.

6 Work with asbestos in progress – The enclosure, airlock system and other aspects of the area should be regularly checked visually and the results recorded. Air sampling should be carried out in conjunction with such inspections to reassure those outside the work area and to check the procedures of the workers and that the integrity of the enclosure is maintained. These again may be posted prominently near the work site.

7 Removal completed – The work area should be inspected by the analyst/supervisor and if satisfactory visually, an airtest carried out within the area to demonstrate effective decontamination. On completion, the area should be

inspected by representatives of the client and then a permit to remove the enclosure issued. The completed work should be notified to those who were affected and an entry made in the asbestos register if, indeed, one is held.

Assessment

This will identify the area and the need for work to be carried out. It will normally follow a request from the owner of a property or his representative for the work. The initial request may not necessarily call for asbestos to be removed or treated. It therefore becomes incumbent upon those appointed to carry out or supervise the work to assure themselves that asbestos is or is not present.

The area should be inspected with care, taking the necessary steps for personal protection. Clearly until any initial visual inspection is made these will not always be known. Therefore, it is wise to ensure that such an inspection is carried out by an experienced 'competent' person. Should the use of personal protection be necessary care should be taken not to cause alarm to persons in the surrounding areas.

If asbestos is thought to be present, a decision must be made as to the number and location of samples to be taken to obtain a representative selection of the materials present.

If at the time of this initial assessment the surveyor/analyst is of the opinion that the area presents a hazard during the time waiting for work to start, then advice should be given to that effect. Clearly such advice must be confirmed as a matter of urgency as soon as analyses are completed. In the event of such confirmation the area should be placed on restricted access and entry permitted only in controlled circumstances. The definition of asbestos area or respirator zone should be made.

Specification of work

The specification will fall into two sections, first the general conditions of contract and the administrative procedures expected to be followed by the contractor and second, specific conditions as necessary from the client's asbestos policy document, together with the findings of any surveys or assessments carried out in connection with the proposed work.

Unfortunately to date this is all too infrequently not the case. Large numbers of specifications include statements to the effect that 'asbestos may be present in a number of areas; all work shall be carried out in accordance with relevant legislation'. This requires each and every tenderer to carry out his own survey and relies on the contractors' own experience. For specific asbestos removal projects such experience is available, but for many general contractors the clause has been demonstrated not to have adequate impact.

Pre-contract meeting

Once a contractor has been appointed, the pre-contract meeting should be called in sufficient time before work actually starts and should be attended by the supervisor, contractor and representatives of both staff and management of the premises where the work is to be carried out. The meeting will thus cover the 'duty to inform' those who may be affected by the work. Typically, the agenda should cover all aspects of the administration and control of the work to be carried out.

- Work area and reasons for carrying out the work.
- Other areas which may be affected by the work, e.g. surrounding corridors to be used for transit routes or waste removal.
- Access to and from the work area to include location and installation of decontamination facilities.
- Procedures to be followed by the contractor in relation to his work and those affected by it. This should include discussion of the method of work statement.
- Emergency procedures, even though they may not be required.
- Notification to the authorities, i.e. Health and Safety Executive, fire brigade, environmental health officers as applicable.

   – Duties of the analyst who will carry out air sample monitoring and clearance testing.
   – Disposal of the waste.

Minutes of the meeting should be taken and circulated to interested parties and, if applicable, to notice boards.

Permit to set up site

This is provided as an aide memoire to both supervisor and contractor at the time he arrives on site to set up the work. Table 7.1 is an example of a typical permit which, when posted at the work site will advise all persons that work is about to commence.

Table 7.1

Permit to set up site (including enclosure) – permit A

Date:
Contractor:
Site:
Job title:
Reference number:

This permit is issued to set up site and enclosures only. No other work shall commence until written authority given by the supervising officer. This permit shall not be issued if full details are not available.

1 Copy of contractors' licence available on site.
2 Copy of medical certificates as issued by medical advisor for all strippers allocated to the site.
3 Method statement available and approved.
4 All persons or departments affected have been advised.
5 Types of asbestos – amosite, chrysotile, crocidolite, others.
6 Health and Safety Executive has been notified.
7 Special equipment necessary:

(*a*) Approved RPE
(*b*) overalls disposable/working/transit/colour
(*c*) vacuum cleaners
(*d*) negative pressure air units
(*e*) labelled wastebags
(*f*) decontamination facility
(*g*) others.

8 Name of contractor representative issued with permit.
9 Period for which permit is issued.
10 Nature of enclosures and agreed positions.
11 Identification of area and prevention of unauthorized entry.
12 Waste disposal
   – Who will dispose of the waste?
   – Temporary storage location.
13 Air monitoring
   – Name of firm.
   – Frequency of tests.
14 Signature of supervisor.
15 Signature of permit holder.

Inspection of enclosure and permit to work

When the contractor has completed his enclosure and set up site in accordance with the method statement and permit to set up site the enclosure should be inspected visually to ensure that there are no obvious holes such as lift shafts or service ducts. In most projects this could entail inspection inside the enclosure as well as outside and all necessary safety precautions should be taken by the inspector who should preferably be experienced in the matter. If an independent analyst or consultant is appointed this inspection in detail can be carried out by him. All areas where pipes pass through walls, other openings etc., should be sealed, but there should also be a controlled air inlet point which will normally be through airlocks or the decontamination train. Without this there is the possibility of collapse of the enclosure due to the section erected by the extract system.

It is in everyone's best interest that this inspection is

satisfactory in the first instance and, therefore, the contractor should make his own inspection prior to the 'official' one. The enclosure and entry/exit system should conform to the various advice and guidance and include all necessary warning signs, barriers, air extraction, decontamination facilities and other ancillary equipment.

Following a satisfactory visual inspection the enclosure should be submitted to a smoke test. A non-toxic dense smoke is fed into the work zone usually by means of a smoke generator which produces a mist of vegetable or other light oil having similar particle size to airborne asbestos fibres. 'Firework' smoke bombs or canisters can be used but they are more difficult to remove from the area and will block the extract system filters, whereas the generator smoke will not normally have this effect. The air extract system should be turned off whilst the smoke test is carried out.

All surrounding areas should then be checked to ensure that no smoke leaks from the work area. In multi-floored buildings it will not be adequate to inspect only the floor above the work zone. Smoke has been found two or more floors up a building to which it has been carried by service riser ducts. Also, where there may be false ceilings or panelling, even the air gap between external walls, smoke has been found to travel from an incorrectly sealed enclosure.

Clearly, it will not always be possible to produce a 100 per cent smoke tightness and it may be necessary to demonstrate that leaks are stopped once the air extract is in commission. Any leaks which cannot be stopped prior to commissioning of the air extract should be noted and the location used for sites of confirmatory air sample monitoring during the work.

When the enclosure is complete, as far as reasonably practical, the permit to work will be issued. Note that the permit (see Table 7.2) includes limits of asbestos fibre concentration at which certain actions will be taken. These levels are well below the statutory control limits, but experience will show that once leaks or bad practices occur, the margin between good and bad results is in fact very small. Therefore, it is wise to take action earlier rather than later.

Table 7.2

Certificate of inspection of enclosure (permit to work with asbestos) permit B

Date:
Contractor:
Site:
Job title:
Reference number:

This is to certify that the asbestos work enclosure has been inspected by analyst/employer/contractor and that a satisfactory smoke test has been carried out to establish the integrity of the enclosure.

The enclosure and air extraction equipment are of satisfactory duty for the work with asbestos to commence.

Short duration leak tests will be carried out following commencement of work with asbestos.

The following action limits will apply resulting from air testing, based on a background count of less than 0.01 fibres/ml.

Asbestos fibre concentration Fibres/ml.		*Action*
0.01	(a)	Cause of leak investigated.
	(b)	Confirmatory short duration sampling.
	(c)	Asbestos workers advised to check procedures and internal seals.
0.02	(a)	Work stopped to find leak and correct.
	(b)	Work restarted when air tests return to less than 0.01 fibres/ml.

Permit to work	– issued by:	Position:
	– issued to:	Position:
	Time:	

A typical permit to work will be in the form of Table 7.2. On large installations, such as power stations or large warehouses, smoke testing may not be practical in the above terms. However, there may well be strategic points where it would be advantageous to check the enclosure, e.g. at exhaust ducting leading to chimney stacks or at roof level near the fanlights. Also, it will not always be practical to put the whole structure under negative pressure since the volume of air to be extracted and filtered would be enormous at the recommended eight to ten air changes per hour. In these cases, air sampling should be carried out inside the work area and procedures such as wet stripping used to limit the evolution of dust.

Air extraction should be applied at all points of extra entry to the asbestos work zone so that clear air is drawn into the entry/exit train from clean sections through the dirty sections. This directional flow will tend to sweep away any fibres from the external environment.

This function will be further dealt with in Chapter 10.

Work with asbestos in progress

Those taking part in the work must ensure their procedures and work area are such as to ensure the safety of those not connected with the work. It is not sufficient to assume that because the enclosure was inspected before the start of work with asbestos and was proved satisfactory it will remain so. Wind, vandals or other outside influences may well affect the integrity of the enclosure, but unless there is a major breach, the air extract system will normally prevent leakage. Nevertheless, regular visual inspections should be made and recorded, particularly when work has stopped for breaks and is about to restart. These routine inspections should be recorded by the contractor's supervisor, analyst or other competent person. The entry and exit air locks should be kept in a clean and tidy condition in order to prevent asbestos from being carried out of the work area.

Readings of the negative pressure exerted by the air extract should also be taken regularly and automatic equipment is available for this. However, when polythene sheeting is used to form the enclosure, adequate negative pressure will obviously cause this to pull inwards.

In the event that the proper conditions are not maintained corrections should be made immediately.

In addition to the visual checks, monitoring of the air outside the enclosure, particularly at the entry/exit and at the exhaust of the air extract, will confirm that correct procedures are being maintained. The results of such air tests should be recorded and exhibited along with other documentation.

Removal work completed

When the contractor has completed the removal of asbestos to his own satisfaction, he will advise the independent analyst to that effect. The work area will then be examined by the analyst, taking full personal protective precautions on the basis that the area has not been declared suitable for unrestricted access.

This examination will be carried out prior to the placing of air samples to determine residual airborne contamination, if any. The inspection will be in detail and will examine all work areas and surfaces for cleanliness, in particular:

- all fixings such as nuts and bolts, rivets, pipe hangers and supports;
- blind spots on pipework such as the inside of bends and the back of pipework when it runs along a wall;
- points where pipework passes through walls;
- nooks and crannies where asbestos could have been missed, including between cables, on cable or other supports;
- screw holes where ceilings have been removed, etc.
- the area should be dry. This may sometimes be difficult in areas where pipework leaks are frequent. However, leaks will generally only affect the floor. In this case the analyst must assure himself that the area is as dry as reasonably practical and that any water remaining is clean and without debris.

Assuming that the area has been cleaned to the satisfactory level, air tests will then be carried out (see Chapter 10). These tests must ensure that there is no airborne asbestos fibre present, nor any which may become airborne during subsequent use of the work area. Thus some method of disturbance will be used which will release any loose fibres from the surfaces but without creating fibre in its own right.

The air extract system must be turned off during such clearance testing.

Provided that inspection and air tests are satisfactory the analyst will then issue a certificate of inspection on completion which incorporates a permit to remove the enclosure. If unsatisfactory results are obtained the certificate should be issued to advise the contractor but no permit. Table 7.3 shows a typical certificate and permit.

Table 7.3

Certificate of inspection on completion (permit to remove enclosure) – Permit C

Date:
Contractor:
Site:
Job title:
Reference number:

A *Failed*
   This is to certify that the area has been inspected on reported completion of work with asbestos, but the work is not satisfactory:
   (*a*) obvious residual material was noted as listed below
   (*b*) air test results.
   The area shall be further cleaned and then reinspected and tested before issue of the permit.

Issued by: Position:

Received by: Position:

B *Acceptable*

This is to certify that the work area has been inspected on reported completion of work with asbestos and the work is satisfactory:

(a) no obvious residual material was noted and the work with asbestos has been carried out satisfactorily

(b) air test results.

The area is cleared for client inspection/removal of enclosure.

Issued by: Position:

Received by: Position:

Application of the procedures

The procedures set out above will apply in all cases where asbestos insulation or asbestos coatings are involved. Experience also shows that for all internal work with asbestos insulation board and generally for asbestos cement the enclosure and controls should be provided.

Whilst it is often thought that the latter materials contain low levels of asbestos and can be removed without breakage, air tests taken during such work will frequently show fibre counts approaching the control limits. Breakage of asbestos insulation board or asbestos cement will give fibre concentration well above the control limits.

For external work with asbestos cement, e.g. on roofs etc., provided the material is wetted and removed without breakage, very low fibre counts are obtained even when using personal sampling techniques.

Chapter 8

ASBESTOS CONTROL
– THE ANALYST

The analyst has a prime duty in most aspects of asbestos control. At the assessment stage he must act with the surveyor or carry out the duties of the surveyor provided that he has relevant experience. He will then prepare and identify the asbestos content of the samples.

At the removal stage he will carry out air tests around the work area during removal work and on clearance testing. This work will be in accordance with Guidance Note EH10 issued by the Health and Safety Executive. Under the Control of Asbestos at Work Regulations analysts who carry out air sample counting are recommended to be accredited by NATLAS (National Laboratory Accreditation Service). Accreditation carries a prerequisite that such laboratories are participants in the RICE (Regular Interlaboratory Counting Exchange) scheme.

RICE

The RICE scheme is operated by the Institute of Occupational Medicine for the Committee of Asbestos Measurement. Its aim is to provide a comparison of performance between laboratories and individual counters in those laboratories and to relate those performances to an automatic counting system, Magiscan.

The Institute of Occupational Medicine has prepared numbers of permanent slides which it circulates at approximately three-monthly intervals. The participating laboratories are divided into groups of around five. Each group will analyse the same batch of slides on each circulation. The results are determined as fibre density – fibres per square millimetre – and returned to the institute for comparison. The results are reported in comparison with other laboratories in the group and against Magiscan. Based on the results obtained against Magiscan the laboratory and thereby the individual counters can be given a performance rating. Each result compares the laboratory calculated fibre density against that determined by Magiscan. The laboratory then receives its rating based on these ratios.

Until August 1987 the performance was determined against the following ranges of results:

Laboratory	Less than	0.45
Magiscan		0.45-3.80
		0.65-2.60
	Greater than	3.80

From August 1987 once the system had obtained better comparison between laboratories the ranges were narrowed to:

	Less than	0.55
		0.55-2.20
		0.70-1.70
	Greater than	2.20

Laboratory classification is determined by the number of results within the various bands. Grades 1 and 2 are rated satisfactory:

Grade 1   75% of results within the first band
Grade 2   75% of results within the second band

Grade 3 is classified as unsatisfactory.

Laboratories are given formal classification after completion of four rounds of slides, those who have not completed four rounds are listed as 'Awaiting classification'.

The classifications listed for those laboratories who have completed four or more rounds are 'Satisfactory' and 'Not satisfactory'. It is unlikely that any laboratory will remain unsatisfactory after the initial one or two rounds.

NATLAS

The National Testing Laboratory Accreditation Scheme forms part of NAMAS, the National Measurement Accreditation Service. This is formed by amalgamation with the British Calibration Service. The two schemes are operated by the National Physical Laboratory.

Under NATLAS, laboratories are assessed, accredited and monitored and under stringent requirements authorized to issue formal certificates and reports for specific types of tests. Their performance is assessed against demonstrated technical and management capability, competence of the staff and the range of facilities. Laboratories must also demonstrate and maintain arrangements for assuring the quality of their work.

Whilst NATLAS accreditation is not obligatory the recent regulations and guidance suggest that it is unlikely that employers with no formal training in the work of measurement of asbestos fibres will be able to do it properly and, in such circumstances the work should be passed to a suitable person or organization. A proven record of accuracy and membership of an appropriate accreditation scheme will be a useful indication of suitability.

Airborne asbestiform fibres

When using optical methods alone, it is not possible to be specific that all fibres collected from the air are asbestos. Therefore the term 'asbestiform' is used to refer to any airborne fibre within the parameters defined for counting.

A countable fibre is defined as any object which is longer than 5µm (micrometres), with a width less than 3µm, and with a length/width ratio of greater than 3:1, which does not touch or appear to touch a particle with a maximum diameter of greater than 3µm.

A split fibre is taken to be one countable fibre if it meets the definition above, otherwise it should be ignored. A split fibre is defined as an agglomerate of fibres which at one or more points on its length appears to be solid and undivided but which at other points appears to divide into separate strands. The width is measured across the undivided part, not the split part.

Fibres in a bundle are counted individually if they can be distinguished sufficiently to meet the definition. If no individual fibres meeting the definition can be distinguished, the bundle is one countable fibre if the bundle as a whole meets the definition.

Sample types

Airborne asbestos fibre sampling is carried out and is necessary to determine whether or not the personal exposure of workers is being controlled to the minimum reasonably practical level. In asbestos removal it also provides evidence of control of the working procedures and enclosures during the removal work.

Air sampling is generally carried out on a static basis using battery-powered sampling pumps which filter the air through cellulose ester filter membrane having a pore diameter of less than 0.8 to 1.2 µm.

In asbestos removal operations, air sampling and determination of asbestiform fibre concentrations are carried out for a number of purposes.

Background samples

For control purposes in subsequent removal works, background samples should be taken in areas outside the designated area of work before such work starts. These will be used to establish a datum to which the later control samples can be related. It must be understood that movement of people and plant in any area can produce airborne fibres which would meet the definition referred to above. Such fibres can be produced by clothing, manmade mineral fibres etc. Thus even if the areas surrounding the designated work area are known to be asbestos free it will still be possible to determine a count of asbestiform fibres. Bearing in mind the close limits which are generally set for monitoring levels outside working enclosures it is essential that a datum level is established. This point is often overlooked and can lead to unnecessary difficulties during the asbestos removal.

Monitoring samples

These may also be referred to as leak tests. The samples are taken outside the working enclosure during asbestos removal work to ensure that the enclosure and procedures used maintain the required standards of cleanliness outside the enclosure.

Tests will also be taken in the hygiene facilities used by the workers to ensure that their personal decontamination procedures are adequate for their own protection.

In large projects such as power station work or where the controlled wet-stripping system is in use, samples will also be taken within the work zone. These are generally at 5-10m from the work face to ensure that wetting and handling of the asbestos is correct.

The requirements for exposure monitoring and minimum practical exposure as required by the Control of Asbestos Regulations appear to put more emphasis on monitoring samples being taken within the enclosure. If this is so it will place an additional burden on the analyst to ensure that he also complies with all relevant procedures when entering and leaving the work area. At present such entry is generally required only for final inspection and clearance on the majority of projects.

Clearance samples

These samples are taken within every enclosure on completion of the work of asbestos removal. They will be taken only when the analyst is satisfied on his visual examination that the area is ready for such air sampling.

Samplers will be set up in the work area in adequate number to take a representative sample of the air within the area. With the samplers operating, the analyst will carry out procedures designed to disturb any asbestos materials or dust left within the area which may not have been evident in his visual inspection.

Personal samples

These are to monitor workers' exposure to asbestos dust and are used in situations where control is required to protect the worker and where procedures may vary from standard. Samples are taken within the worker's breathing zone generally using the battery-powered sampler strapped to the waist and a long tube to the filter in the breathing zone.

Personal sampling can be extremely valuable where workers, outside or inside, are handling asbestos cement materials which are generally considered 'safe'. It can sometimes be difficult for the analyst or supervisor to achieve safe methods of working or protection of the worker without recourse to such sampling.

Sampling volume/time

All samples should be taken over sufficient time or be of sufficient volume to allow counting of any fibres collected and also to allow corrective measures to be taken if necessary before serious contamination occurs.

Background samples are usually taken for not less than two hours or 200-300 litres of air; the same will apply for monitoring samples on smaller projects. On large projects four-hour samples will be taken with not less than 500 litres of air.

Monitoring samples taken within the work zone will be of shorter duration to enable reasonable counting to be carried out. Clearance samples are required to be of not less than 480 litres with a recommendation for 500-1000 litres. Personal samples should be taken to represent the exposure of the worker over a typical working period generally not less than 2 hours.

Fibre counting equipment

Asbestiform fibre counting is carried out by microscopic examination of the fibres collected during sampling with the cellulose ester filter membrane.

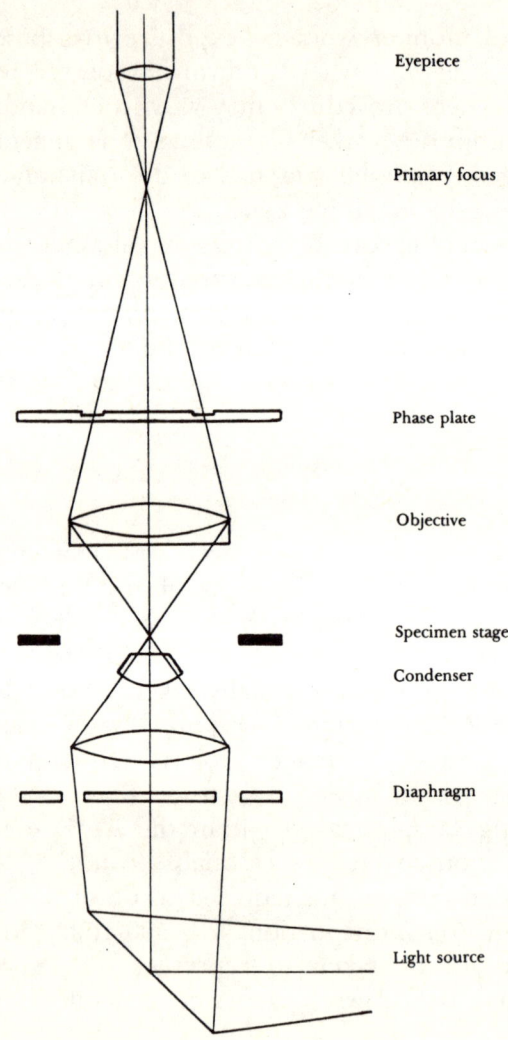

Figure 8.1   *Optical layout of a phase contrast microscope, showing Koehler illumination*

The microscope should be a binocular instrument using phase contrast optics and having Koehler or Koehler-type illumination with a magnification of approximately 500 times (see Figure 8.1). Provided that the objective is a 40 times positive phase contrast achromatic type, minor changes in the microscope specification may not affect the results. However, the microscope must be such that band 5 can be seen on the HSE/NPL phase contrast test slide (see Figure 8.2).

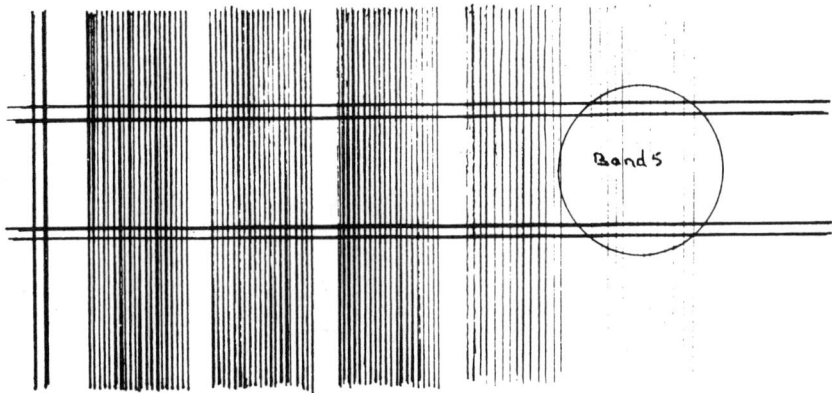

Figure 8.2 *NPL test slide*

The microscope should be fitted with a Walton and Beckett-type eyepiece graticule which must be made for the instrument with which it is to be used. It should have an apparent diameter when checked with a stage micrometer of between 98 and 102μm but a diameter of between 96μm and 104μm is probably satisfactory (see Figure 8.3).

Each time the microscope is set up for fibre counting it should be correctly adjusted and checked both with the HSE/NPL test slide and with the stage micrometer. Under the requirements of NATLAS the stage micrometer should itself be calibrated regularly against a master stage micrometer which has been certified by the National Physical Laboratory.

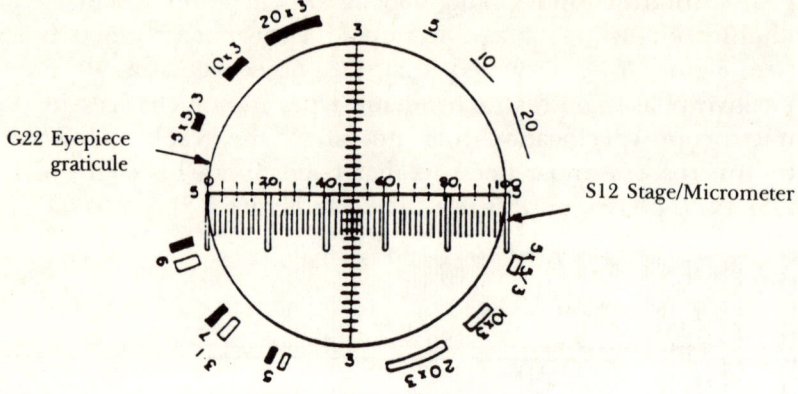

Figure 8.3   *Calibration of Walton/Beckett graticule*

Preparation of the sample for analysis

The filter membrane is removed carefully from the sampling head with flat-nosed forceps and placed on the microscope slide. Several procedures may be used to clear the filter for examination. The most general to date has been the glycerol-triacetate method, in which the filter membrane is placed onto a drop of the solvent already on the slide. After adding a cover slip, the slide is gently heated to dissolve the membrane and clear the slide. This method is only for semi-permanent slides.

Permanent slides can be prepared using acetone vapour. This method until recently was not suitable for use outside full-scale laboratories due to the flammability of acetone, but recent developments for acetone vapour generation specific to the requirements have made this possible.

Alternatively permanent slides may be prepared with a mixture of DMF/Eupural. However, these chemicals are hazardous and again cannot be widely used on site situations.

When the slide has been cleared it is placed on the microscope and analysed by counting the total of asbestiform fibres in a number of graticule areas. This number is converted to fibres/ml by calculation using the formula

$$\frac{\text{Asbestiform fibre}}{\text{Concentration fibres/ml}} = \frac{1000ND^2}{Vn\,d^2}$$

where N is the number of fibres counted

n is the number of graticule areas examined

D mm is the diameter of the exposed area of the filter membrane

d μm is the diameter of the Walton-Beckett graticule as measured with the stage micrometer

V litres is the volume of air sampled.

D, the diameter of the exposed area of the filter membrane is measured by taking a sample from a cloud of dark coloured dust using the standard sampling equipment. The filter membrane is then prepared and mounted in the standard manner. The prepared slide is then examined at low magnification whilst traversing the diameter of the darkened area. The diameter can then be measured from the vernier scale of the microscope.

Based on the counting principles set out previously the analyst will then determine the number of fibres using the counting rules as follows:

- at least 100 fibres must be counted (where this number are present);
- a minimum of 20 graticule areas must be examined;
- at low concentration as will be found on clearance samples 200 graticule areas should be counted;
- for external monitors during asbestos removal a compromise may be acceptable to limit the number of graticule areas examined to 100 provided that this is documented in the laboratory in house procedures.

Examples of counting principles are shown in Figure 8.4.

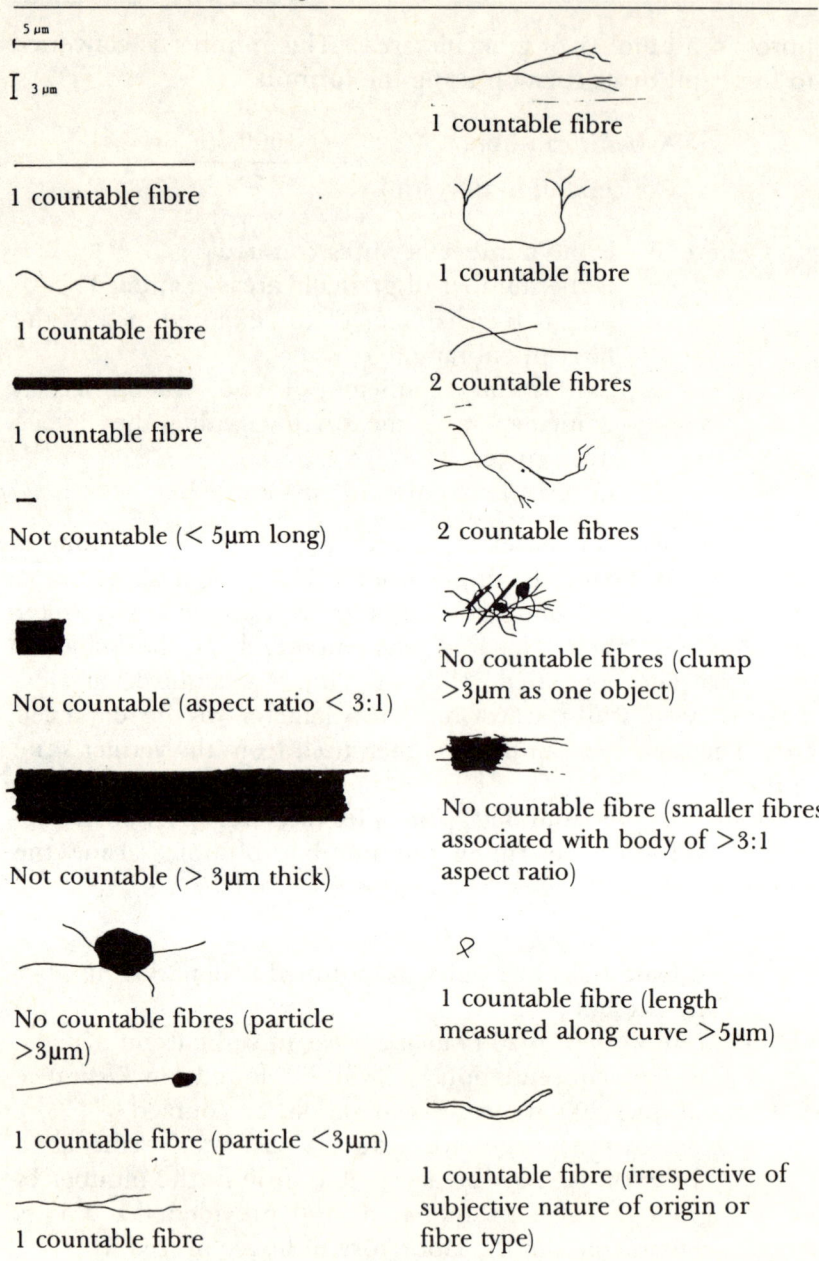

Figure 8.4 *Counting principles of asbestiform fibres*

Graticure diameter
eg 100 µm

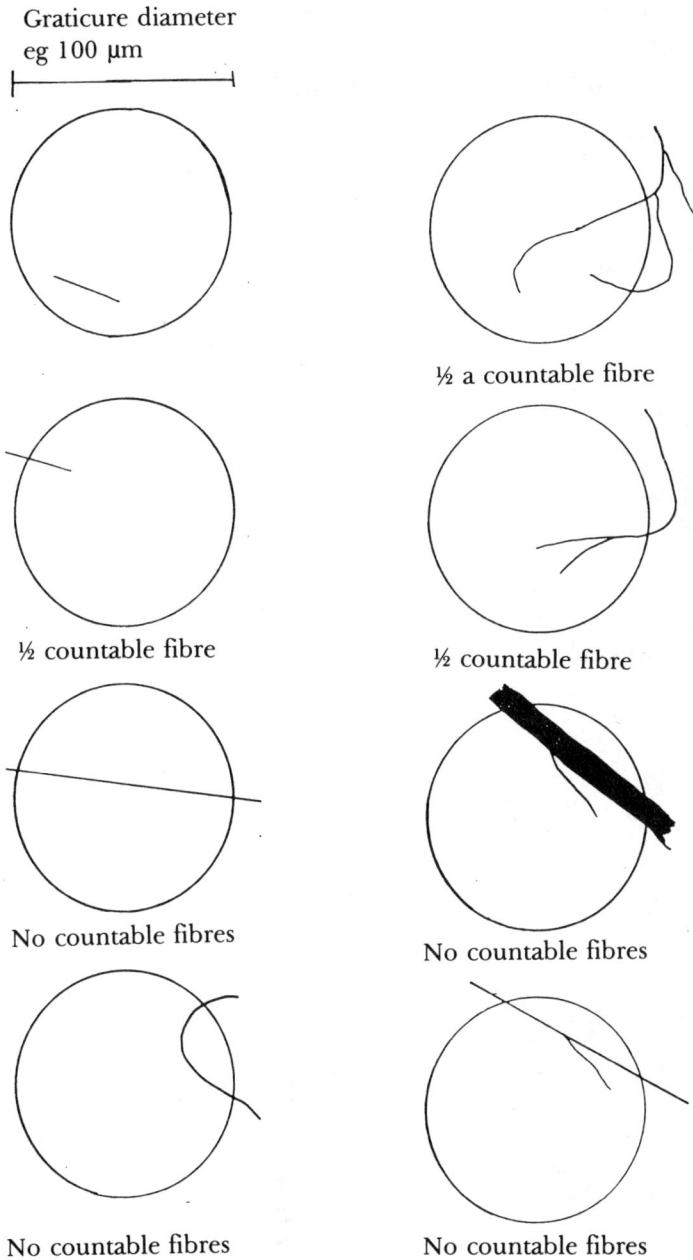

½ a countable fibre

½ countable fibre

½ countable fibre

No countable fibres

No countable fibres

No countable fibres

No countable fibres

Figure 8.4   *Counting principles of asbestiform fibres (continued)*

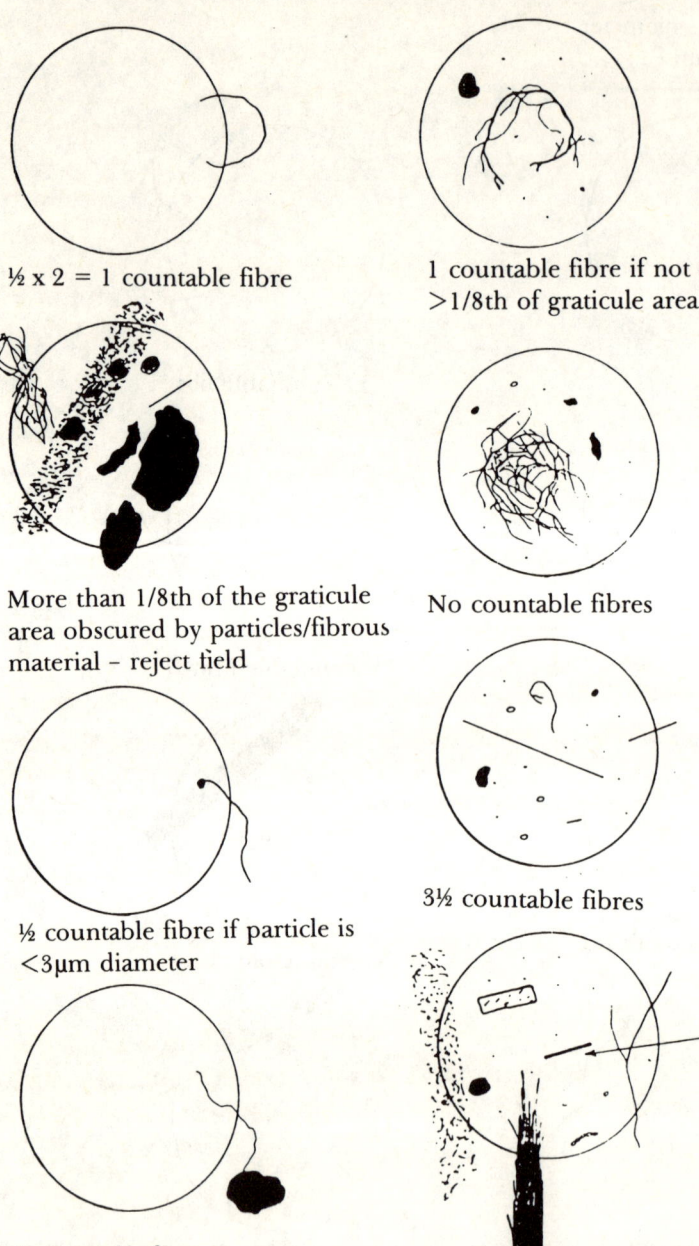

½ x 2 = 1 countable fibre

1 countable fibre if not occupying >1/8th of graticule area

More than 1/8th of the graticule area obscured by particles/fibrous material – reject field

No countable fibres

½ countable fibre if particle is <3μm diameter

3½ countable fibres

No countable fibres

1 countable fibre

Figure 8.4   *Counting principles of asbestiform fibres (concluded)*

Quality control

All laboratories should operate an internal quality control programme to maintain their consistency and comparability.

Those laboratories in the RICE scheme do this already but individual laboratories can develop an internal system amongst their own analysts on a comparable basis. Obviously this will not include correlation against Magiscan. However, if the RICE slides are treated in the same manner as the internal system, the individual results can be used in the internal system. This will then correlate the internal results against Magiscan.

All such quality control results should be recorded and the individual performances logged to ensure that the overall standards remain comparable and satisfactory.

Analysis of Bulk Samples

General

Unless contractors accept the premise that all asbestos will be classified as crocidolite, they need to be advised of the type of asbestos present in the material to be handled.

Equally, when surveying for Asbestos Register information, the type of asbestos present may affect the recommendation made for action. Therefore, in planning work with asbestos the assessment should include identification of the type and approximate percentage content of the asbestos present.

The analysis procedure should be carried out only in laboratories which are equipped for the handling of asbestos and its products. The facilities should include fume cabinets with filtered dust exhaust or an environmental cabinet designed for the purpose.

The analysts must also be aware of the potential risks of exposure to asbestos fibres.

Observation

A visual examination will indicate to the experienced analyst the likely general classification and content of the material, as listed in Chapter 5.

Preparation for analysis

Loosely-bound compounds can often be separated adequately to allow microscopic examination. Well-bonded compounds will require chemical or mechanical preparation. Chemicals used include acids for cement products, e.g. dilute cold hydrochloric or hot dilute acetic acid. Caustic soda may be used to separate diatomaceous earth or organic binders.

When chemical methods are used the resultant mixture should be sieved using a fine mesh and rinsed with water. The recovered fibres may then be dried for identification.

In some instances, for example with cement boards, drilling, filing or scraping will provide adequate fibres for analysis.

The sample of 'mixed' fibres obtained can be separated and a preliminary identification obtained using a stereo microscope at about 40 times magnification. This will also allow assessment of the relative proportions of the various types. The types should be separated and samples placed on microscope slides for further inspection.

For quantitative estimation of the asbestos content, samples should be weighed before and after chemical treatment to remove the fillers and binders, at the same time making allowance for asbestos lost during the sieving process if the total asbestos content is required.

Identification of asbestos type

Confirmation of type is obtained by further inspection of the fibres selected from the preliminary work using the stereo microscope.

Identification is then carried out using the dispersion staining technique. This involves examination of the fibres in a suitable immersion liquid under a cover slip using polarized light. The method uses the differences in refractive index for the different types of asbestos to give a range of colours specific to asbestos type when viewed using polarized light.

Both amosite and crocidolite oxidize to a brown colour when heated. This occurs at 400°C for crocidolite and 600°C for amosite. The change in colour is accompanied by changes in the crystal structure which also changes the refractive index. In this situation the dispersion staining procedure can no longer apply.

Other methods such as X-ray diffraction must then be used for full identification.

Chapter 9

ASBESTOS REMOVAL
– THE CONTRACTOR

Prior to the Asbestos (Licensing) Regulations 1983 it was technically acceptable for anyone to carry out asbestos removal work, so long as he followed the approved code of practice or the various guidance notes.

The Asbestos (Licensing) Regulations provide for work with asbestos insulation and coatings to be carried out only under licence issued by the Health and Safety Executive. Such licence requires that the contractor accepts certain obligations. The main criterion, apart from working in compliance with the code of practice, is that all those who work with asbestos insulation or coatings shall be under medical surveillance.

The Control of Asbestos at Work Regulations increase these obligations to include on a formal basis the training of operators, examination of equipment and facilities and the keeping of records relating to such. Further, and from a practical point of view, the requirement for a specific written method statement for each job is of importance.

In the past some contractors have prepared a standard method statement for submission with their proposal for the work and this has met the basic regulatory requirements. However, few actual jobs on site are standard and it is left to those on site to decide how to set up the job. Unless the work has been properly planned difficulties can be experienced when equipment or materials are not available as required.

Assessment

The contractor should have been provided with a specification and survey indicating the extent of work required. If this is not available he has an obligation to make his own assessment. Contractually this is in his own interests and should clearly define his extent of work and supply.

Based on this assessment the contractor will visit the site to estimate and record for his own purposes the materials, equipment, personnel, availability of services and waste disposal arrangements required to carry out the work in the most expeditious and economic fashion. He should also include specific instructions to his work force on the method of work.

Notification

As soon as possible the contractor must notify the Health and Safety Executive of his appointment to carry out the work. This is obligatory for any work with asbestos insulation, asbestos coating or crocidolite. Where other materials are to be handled notification may not be obligatory but is nevertheless advisable. In demolition and refurbishment, the requirement for advising the executive is included in the relevant guidance notes.

Information to employees

No employee should be put to work on asbestos without a general training course to inform him of the obligations relating to asbestos. Lack of such training can give rise to personal risk, risk to his work mates and risk to the public and to the company. Further, provision of the method of work statement referred to above will provide information to employees detailed to carry out specific work. They should maintain a copy of the statement in their site documentation.

Method statement

It is not intended here to provide a typical method statement, but the points noted below should be included by the contractor for use by his staff in the execution of the work. The list prepared as an aide memoire should avoid most of the pitfalls which have been noted.

1 Client and contract.
2 Site address and, if necessary, detailed directions.
3 Architect/engineer/supervisor/analyst.
4 Location of work on site.
5 Asbestos materials and type of asbestos to be removed.
6 Work area and enclosure including siting of decontamination facilities.
7 Work procedures – method of removal of asbestos; safe access platforms if required; waste disposal; air monitoring and analyst.
8 Equipment required.
9 Decontamination facilities and procedures.
10 Waste disposal arrangements.
11 Emergency procedures.
12 Documentation.

Where a pre-contract meeting is held, this will form the basis of the contractor's presentation.

Setting up site

On arrival at site, the foreman should locate the client contact and set up his compound as has been agreed previously.

Dependent on the assessment of the work and status of the work area given in the method statement the crew should then commence to set up the work enclosure. Priority should be given to welfare and decontamination facilities since the setting up of a work enclosure can lead to release of asbestos thereby requiring decontamination.

The site and work area should be marked clearly by ropes and barriers with statutory warning signs against unauthorized entry.

All moveable items should be removed from the work area, if necessary, following decontamination. All fixed items not requiring asbestos removal should be covered with polythene sheeting to prevent contamination during the work.

The enclosure should then be set up, using polythene sheeting, self-adhesive tape, spray adhesive, expanding foam, cement mortar or other materials to seal all obvious holes, cracks and openings. The polythene sheeting should generally be not less than 500 gauge but preferably 1000 gauge. In practice the adhesive tape is best at 2–3 inches width. For external work reinforced polythene and tape or wooden battens are recommended.

Experience has shown that enclosures should be provided for all asbestos removal work carried out inside buildings whether it be insulation, which is obligatory, asbestos insulation board or asbestos cement. The handling of broken board products in the dry state will give rise to airborne asbestos fibre counts approaching or exceeding the control limits. For external work it is not always practical and certainly not economic to use enclosures at all times. However, the procedures used must then take account of this fact and should be monitored to ensure that asbestos release is kept as low as reasonably practical, particularly when working with asbestos cement sheeting. For pipework or vessels, enclosure and/or control at source must be practised.

The negative pressure air extraction unit or units should be put in place during the setting up of the enclosure as should the entry/exit system. All equipment should be tested to ensure that it functions correctly.

Where the work area to be enclosed is considered or known to be subject to airborne contamination, the entry/exit and decontamination systems must be put in place first. They should be used with the necessary personal protective equipment.

Once the enclosure and installation of equipment is completed, the contractor should carry out his own inspection before offering to the supervisor. The enclosure will then be smoke tested as described previously before work is commenced.

Figure 9.1 shows two different typical small project enclosures.

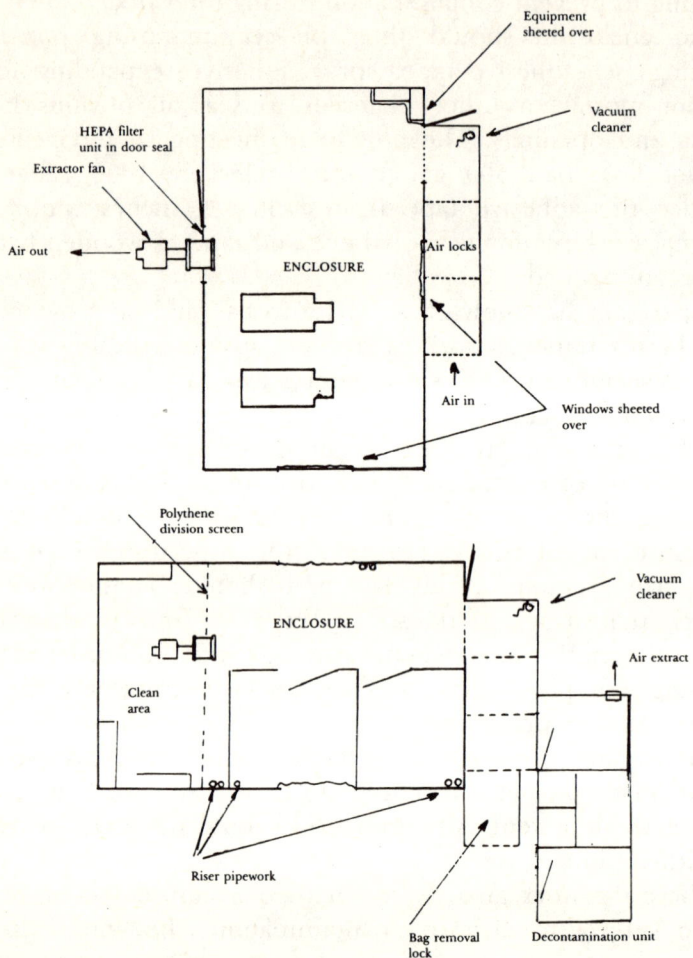

Figure 9.1   *Typical small project enclosures*

On large sites particularly the work area should be cleaned as far as possible before work starts with asbestos. This is particularly true on demolition projects, when frequently the premises may have been standing for some time and where the last occupant will generally have left considerable quantities of rubbish.

Air sampling may be necessary and is in any case advisable during this setting-up period to ensure that those carrying out the work are correctly equipped with personal protective equipment or to justify it not being necessary.

The enclosure should allow for emergency exit, particularly in large areas or in confined spaces such as ducts.

Working methods

Methods of work within the enclosure should be arranged to minimize the evolution of dust as far as possible. Asbestos should be placed in bags as it is removed to avoid it spreading or being tramped in to the floor.

The area should be worked in a logical fashion so that cleaned sections are not recontaminated by subsequent work.

Where there are hot pipes or vessels start work near to the air exhaust point and work back towards the entry/exit. In this manner, the hottest air is being drawn away from the work. However, the contractor should be aware of the potential problems associated with heat stress and should have made allowance for these in his method statement and his original scope of supply.

Full decontamination procedures must be followed each and every time the workers leave the enclosure, and at the end of the day's work or shift all asbestos which has been removed should be collected, bagged and removed from the area to load into the skip. Efficient working is not possible if the enclosure is stacked with waste bags or if quantities of waste are allowed to build up unbagged on the floor.

All waste should be double bagged, labelled and placed in the waste skip which should be kept locked when not in use. Notification for disposal of the waste must be made on the waste disposal form (s. 17, Control of Pollution Act) at least three days before the skip is moved off site. This is to allow the administrative procedures to be followed through within the waste disposal authorities.

Procedures must comply with all aspects of health and safety legislation, not merely asbestos. Too frequently the procedures for safe access to work, electrical regulations etc., appear to be given scant attention.

Decontamination facilities

The contractor must provide decontamination facilities appropriate to the work. On most projects this comprises a mobile caravan with clean, shower and dirty compartments.

Wherever possible this facility should be connected directly to the work area. Where it is not possible a preliminary decontamination facility must be provided, generally a wooden or metal framework covered with polythene sheeting. The division of clean, 'shower', dirty, is created with polythene sheeting and flaps to maintain the three separate areas. This facility is referred to as the airlocks and is used with a transit procedure to the main facility.

All personnel and waste materials must enter and leave the area through the main or transit decontamination facilities. The decontamination procedures and equipment are dealt with in Chapter 10. This is an important aspect of the occupational safety and hygiene requirements of work with asbestos.

For outside work on non-insulation projects, e.g. removal of asbestos cement roofing sheets, the mobile decontamination facility must be provided and the operators should use it at times when work has stopped. Asbestos cement sheet, even though generally containing a low concentration of asbestos and being largely chrysotile (white asbestos), will soften and erode with age.

Chapter 10

DECONTAMINATION FACILITIES AND PROCEDURE

All work with asbestos products requires close attention to decontamination facilities and procedures. It will have been seen from previous chapters that only the most stringent control of the spead of airborne asbestos fibres can be accepted. No controls will totally eliminate airborne asbestiform fibres and therefore the procedures and equipment must be designed to provide the maximum security and minimum practical levels to which workers are subjected.

For some time, there has been an hypothesis that mesothelioma can be caused by a single asbestos fibre. This is due to the absence of a proven 'non-effect' threshold exposure level for asbestos-related lung cancer. However, work in Canada supports the claim that asbestos has no appreciable effect at low doses. The risk rises dramatically only at higher cumulative exposure. In terms of cumulative dose, the threshold for increased risk of lung cancer from exposure to asbestos appears to be in the range 25-100 fibre/ml years. The Ontario Royal Commission suggests 25 fibre/ml years as a threshold for clinical asbestosis.

The control of Asbestos at Work Regulations 1987 introduce action leads to supplement control limits. These set accumulated exposure levels at 48 fibre hours/ml for amosite and crocidolite and 120 fibre hours/ml for other types over any 12-week period. For mixed exposures a proportionate number applies.

Requirements of decontamination facilities

Based on the requirement to achieve minimum practical levels of exposure to the workers and to prevent release of asbestos fibres to the outside environment, all decontamination areas should include the following facilities.

There must be at least three separate areas comprising clean, decontamination by shower, etc., dirty.

Clean area

An area for removing and storing all clothing worn to work. This should be large enough to accept the work force during the times of going to and from work. It should be provided with seating and hygiene arrangements as well as secure separate lockers for each worker's clothes and valuables which cannot be taken into the work area.

Decontamination/shower area

The shower area should have adequate facilities to accommodate the work force in a reasonable time. Generally no more than three persons should be allocated to one shower cubicle unless staggered working times are arranged.

All water discharge from the shower area should pass through a fine filter to prevent loss of asbestos to the receiving system. The area should have running hot and cold water or warm water, soap, shampoo, nail brushes and clean towels.

Dirty area

An area for removing and replacement of protective clothing and respiratory protective equipment together with a means of storing such equipment in lockers or at least on hooks. A mirror should be provided for the worker to see that he has correctly fitted his respiratory protective equipment.

There should be a flow of clean air through all sections to prevent the movement of contaminated air towards the clean side of the facility. This is done by means of an air extraction unit placed in the dirty area which draws air from the clean end of the facility.

Doors between each section should be self closing and only one door should be opened at any one time. Each door will be fitted with air flow louvres to allow controlled passage of air under the influence of the air extractor. Wherever possible to assist in the prevention of contamination of the clean areas, the whole facility should be laid out in such a way that workers are deterred from returning to the dirty conditions area once they have decontaminated themselves. For examples of layout of decontamination units see Figure 10.1.

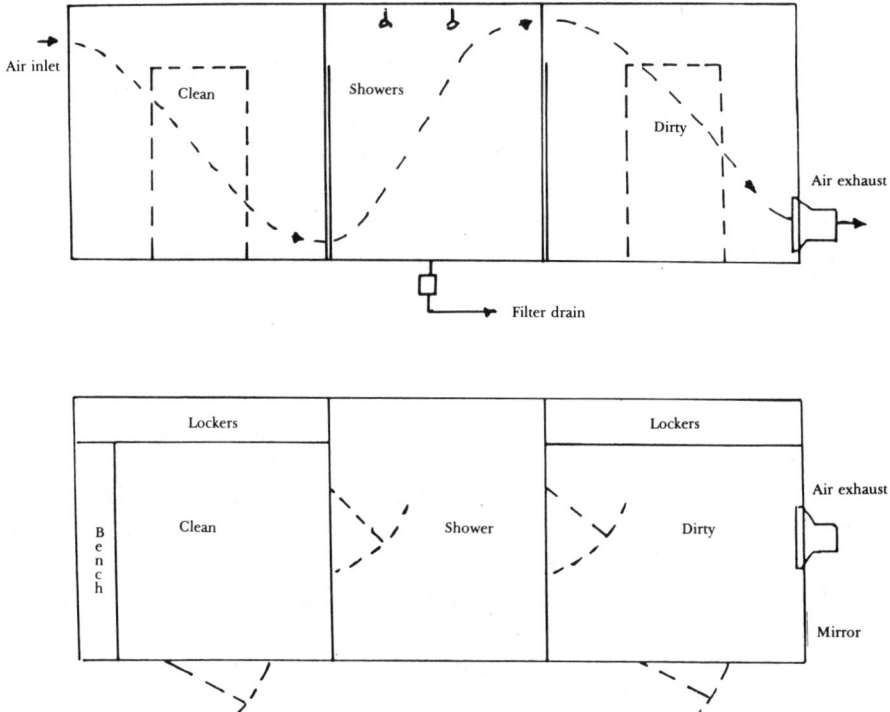

Figure 10.1 *Decontamination units*

Location of facilities

Decontamination facilities as described should, wherever possible, be joined directly to the asbestos working area to prevent contamination of other areas. Where this is not possible, supplementary facilities must be provided attached to the working area and transit procedures developed which protect the workers and prevent risk to others whilst the workers move from the work area to the main decontamination facility.

In many instances, these transit facilities are in fact also used prior to a main facility to assist in the control, even when the main facility could be directly attached to the work area. In either situation the supplementary facility, if used, will reduce the load on the main facility.

The supplementary facility should allow the worker to vacuum clean his protective clothing and equipment, remove and store his protective clothing, wash his hands and the external surfaces of his respiratory protective equipment. If remote from the decontamination unit, the supplementary facility should also allow the worker to change into transit clothing to give him access to the main facility. The working and transit clothing and footwear should be of different colour or specification to avoid confusion.

Main or supplementary facilities should be cleaned regularly at least once a day and probably more frequently, dependent on use.

Air testing should be carried out in the clean areas on a routine basis to ensure that the procedures are correctly followed and that the areas remain clean as specified. On larger installations, air tests carried out in the dirty side of the facilities will assist in maintenance control.

On small projects, purpose-built airlocks may be used with the inclusion of a shower in the central section of the airlock. They are more frequently used for transit decontamination/supplementary facilities and may be constructed from polythene sheeting using wooden or metal frameworks and should include at least three chambers, particularly when working with dusty materials (see Figure 10.2). Recent advice and guidance material, together with developments from equipment suppliers is leading to greater use of modular systems with prefabricated metal frameworks and cubicles to form the airlock unit. Further development from this is the use of glass reinforced plastic modular systems which, though relatively costly, appear economic in the longer term when material and man hour costs are taken into account.

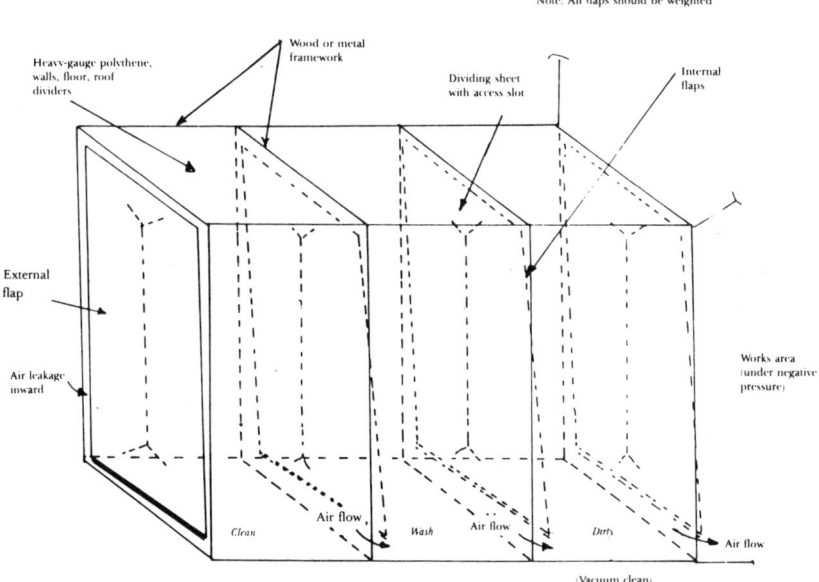

Figure 10.2 *Airlock unit*

Decontamination Procedures

Under the interpretation of the regulations these procedures, or acceptable variations of them, must be used each and every time a person enters or leaves a working enclosure for any reason. For work outside, such as on asbestos cement roofing removal, there may be some reduction in the requirements, but nevertheless decontamination must still be undertaken.

Decontamination unit connected directly to the work area by an airlock

Entry to work area

1   Enter the clean area of the decontamination unit, remove all clothing and store in the lockers or cupboards provided.
2   Put on respiratory protective equipment (RPE) (previously cleaned) but leave the belt hanging if the respirator is the positive powered type.
3   Pass through or past the shower area, without showering.
4   Enter the 'dirty' area of the unit, shutting both internal doors.
5   Put on any underclothing to be worn in the work area. NOTE: Any such underclothing which has been worn in the work area must be considered contaminated and not returned to the clean zones until it has been laundered by an approved laundry.
6   Pass out of the decontamination unit, into the airlock and put on protective clothing, boots and gloves ensuring that the trousers of the coverall are outside the boots, sleeves outside the gloves and hood pulled down to the RPE.
7   Fasten the belt of the RPE and proceed to the work area.

Exit from work area

This procedure must be followed each and every time exit is made from the work area for whatever purpose.

1   At a clean point in the work area and immediately before entering the airlock, clean off boots, gloves and any large deposits of material from the coverall.
2   Enter the first section of the airlock/decontamination train and vacuum off loose fibres from the coverall and RPE taking care to keep the vacuum hose away from filters and valves of the RPE face piece. It may be helpful to work in pairs for the vacuum cleaning operation so that dust can be removed from the back of the coverall.
3   Remove the coverall, keeping the RPE in operation. If the coverall is sufficiently dirty to justify laundering it should be placed in a bag provided for the purpose. If it is to be used

again it should be hung on a hook provided for the purpose. This will prevent any debris being transferred from boots, etc. Remove boots and gloves.

4　Pass into the central section of the airlock or direct to the dirty condition section of the decontamination unit. Remove the underclothes worn below the working coveralls and then immediately prior to entry to the shower unit disconnect the power unit of the RPE. The face piece should be left in place and the suction hose should be plugged to prevent potential contamination of the inside of the hose. This could later be blown into the face piece. Where it is necessary to change a prefilter or main filter, this work should be carried out by one person wearing suitable personal protection.

5　The RPE face piece should be worn into the shower and removed under the shower. It will also be advisable to wash the inside to freshen it. The face piece should be regularly disinfected using a dilute solution of mild disinfectant. It should not be washed with detergents. Whilst in the shower, the worker should pay particular attention to washing his hair and scrubbing his finger nails to remove any trapped asbestos.

6　After showering, pass through to the clean area, dry and dress in everyday clothes.

Care must be taken to ensure that the doors are shut as movement is made from one area to another.

Transit procedure where the decontamination facility is remote from the work area

The procedures as above should be carried out, but additionally transit coveralls should be worn between the airlocks and decontamination facility. These must be treated as contaminated because the wearer has not carried out the full procedure unless he has showered. For the same reasons the full RPE should be worn when in transit. Transit footwear should be provided as that worn in the work area will be contaminated and everyday footwear should not be taken beyond the shower otherwise it will be contaminating the wearer in transit.

In large asbestos removal projects, these procedures and facilities will be modified as illustrated to account for the numbers of persons involved and the duration of the project. The decontamination facility shown in Figure 10.3 has proved totally satisfactory in this duty with 20 or more persons passing through it at a time over a period of 12 months.

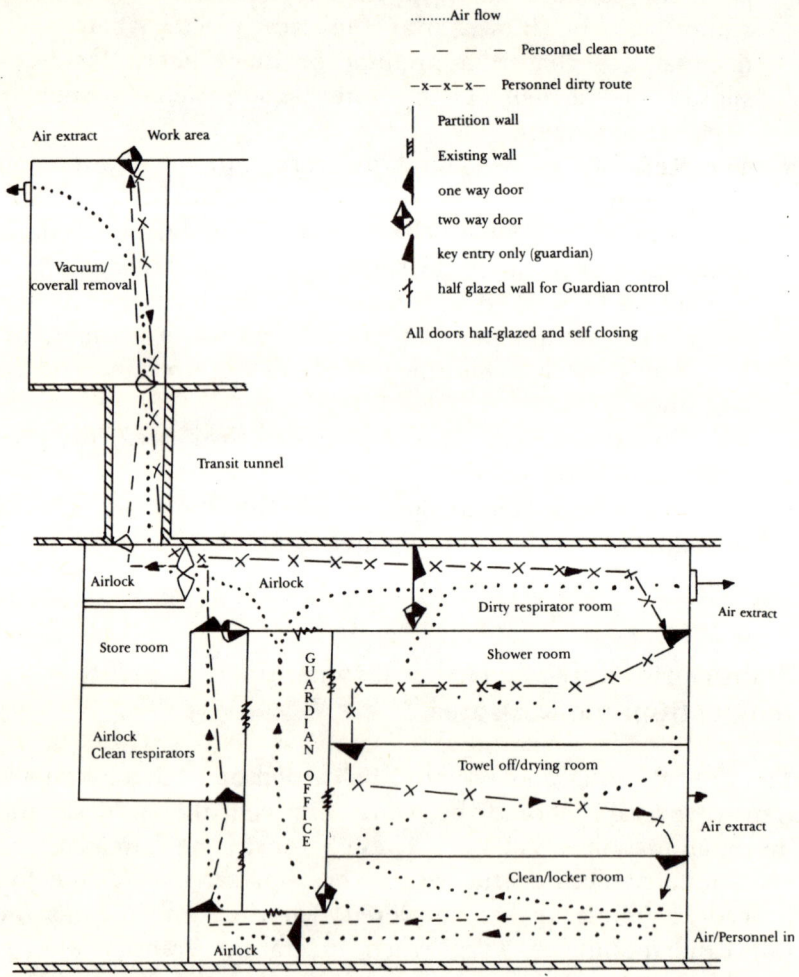

Figure 10.3 *Large-scale decontamination unit*

Chapter 11

PERSONAL PROTECTIVE AND ASSOCIATED EQUIPMENT

In a factory where asbestos products are made it is required and practical to maintain satisfactorily low levels of airborne asbestos fibre concentration. Working practices, fixed machinery and exhaust systems can be geared to maintain the required criteria.

Asbestos removal however, is a transient operation with typical projects lasting only days or weeks. Even major projects such as power stations may extend only for a year or more and cannot be considered permanent installations. The factory situation therefore cannot be applied to asbestos removal.

Thus the workers must be provided with personal protective equipment and the ancillary machinery to give the best reasonably practical protection and minimum dust levels for personal exposure and the control of the working environment.

Enclosure of the working area and the procedures discussed previously provide the mechanical barriers and working practices to achieve the practical control. However, conditions within the work area can never be assumed to meet a level at which personal protection becomes unnecessary. Under the regulations and Health and Safety at Work etc. Act 1974 therefore the requirement for provision and use of personal protective equipment is obligatory.

Respiratory protective equipment

RPE was never intended as a substitute for properly designed and operated ventilation systems which should minimize worker exposure to harmful dusts and fumes. It should be used as a last resort when other methods cannot reasonably achieve the levels required. This is certainly the case with asbestos removal.

RPE should be worn at all times unless testing indicates that adequately low levels of airborne asbestos fibres are being maintained in the immediate work area, i.e. by personal sampling.

RPE falls into two classes:

- respirators in which air from the working environment is drawn through a filter to remove the airborne hazard;
- breathing apparatus in which the wearer is provided with a supply of uncontaminated air from outside the working environment. This independent air supply can be from hoses supplied by a compressor or from bottles carried by the wearer.

Respirators can be fitted with filters specific for dusts such as asbestos or for fumes or gases and it is essential that the correct filter is fitted for the duty.

Workers have been found using solvent-based paints on pipework and vessels previously stripped of asbestos. This painting was being carried out in the enclosure wearing the respirator and filters used for removing the asbestos insulation. Filters used for dust provide no protection whatsoever against fumes or gases or in oxygen-deficient atmospheres. This situation highlights the need for correct training and instruction of workers.

No respirator provides protection against oxygen-deficient atmospheres and must, therefore, never be used in atmospheres immediately dangerous to life. Further dust filters are for use against dust only and are not effective against gases or vapours.

However, fitted with the correct gas or fume filter and provided that the gases or fumes do not create an oxygen-deficient atmosphere, respirators similar to those for dust can be used.

For work in oxygen-deficient atmospheres the RPE provided must be as breathing apparatus.

Dependent upon the work to be carried out, Form 2486 lists the following types of RPE for protection against asbestos:

- half-mask dust respirators
- disposable filtering facepiece respirators
- high efficiency dust respirators fitted with full-face masks
- standard and high efficiency positive powered respirators (including respirators fitted with half masks, full-face masks, half suits and full suits)
- ventilated visor respirators
- breathing apparatus.

Respirators

There is a wide range of respirators available for use with asbestos which can be divided into four broad categories for use under specific conditions.

1   Respirators which require a good seal between the facepiece and the face and which use suction generated by breathing the air through a dust filter and having, usually, one-way inhalation and exhalation valves. The facepiece is a rubber half mask covering only the mouth and nose or is a full-face mask. Disposable facepiece filters are the same shape as the rubber half mask but generally not equipped with exhalation valves.
2   Respirators which depend on a good facepiece fit but to which filtered air is supplied to the wearer by a battery-powered blower. These maintain a positive pressure inside the facepiece and because leakages occur therefore provide a higher degree of protection than the non-powered, negative-pressure types.

3   Hooded blouses or suits to which filtered air is supplied by a powered blower. These may be provided with exhalation valves but generally rely on restriction of air outflow at the waist, wrist and ankles. These can be used to overcome the face fit requirements of the respirators described above.

4   Face visors or helmets to which filtered air is supplied by a powered blower. These again do not rely on a face fit but on the generation of sufficient airflow to maintain a positive pressure within the visor or prevent dust inhalation.

Limitations to work

Working in respiratory protective equipment requires consideration of those who carry out the work. The RPE should be as comfortable as possible and therefore fit as well as is necessary for protection.

Physical and thermal stress must be taken into account and can be the limiting factor depending upon conditions.

All asbestos removal work is labour-intensive, requiring physical effort. In many instances the pipes, or boilers from which pipes are to be stripped, are still hot. Working periods should take account of this and the workers must be given adequate breaks. This becomes exceedingly important at temperatures in excess of 90°F. Experience suggests that exposure to temperatures above 90°F should be avoided if at all possible otherwise work periods as short as 20 minutes should be adopted with a clear break of at least one hour out of the work zone.

Potential clients should be made fully aware of this aspect of the work and the advice will be backed up by the Health and Safety Executive if necessary.

Power-assisted respirators or airlines can ease the potential stress but the heat should be removed if at all possible. Where local cooling cannot be provided work practices should be designed to limit the heat exposure to the workers.

Standards of use

All respiratory protective equipment approved for use with asbestos or other hazards must be approved by the Health and Safety Executive. It is listed in the schedule to the current Certificate of Approval (Respiratory Protective Equipment) published annually by HMSO as Form 2486. Not all equipment listed is suitable for use with asbestos and care should be taken in selection from the equipment as scheduled.

RPE should be issued to individuals as an item of personal protection to be kept by the individual and maintained in good condition with regular checks by a supervisor and with regard to the following standards:

(a) RPE should fit snuggly to the face of the wearer and make a good seal. It will not fit or seal correctly if the wearer has a beard or side whiskers or wears spectacles. In practice a beard should be considered to be more than 24 hours' growth;

(b) the wearer has been trained in the use and maintenance of his RPE and knows its limitations;

(c) the equipment has been correctly issued for the work to be done;

(d) the equipment is maintained and checked to be in a suitable condition for its use.

Care and maintenance

Workers should be advised, and it should be ensured, that no RPE is used by a person other than to whom it was issued unless it has been adequately cleaned and disinfected.

Facepieces should be disinfected, washed and cleaned regularly depending on use.

Visors frequently become scratched and should be replaced so that optimum vision is maintained. It should be appreciated that even with a clear visor, vision will be restricted.

Records should be kept of cleaning and maintenance dates, the dates of issue and the recipients of RPE.

Filters should be replaced regularly dependent on the work being carried out and all used filters should be disposed of as asbestos waste by the procedures approved and documented.

Regular checks of RPE should be carried out to ensure that it is serviceable; straps, valves and facepieces should be checked for wear or signs of deterioration and the necessary remedial measures taken.

Selection of RPE for asbestos removal operations

The Guidance Note EH41 gives as an appendix a simplified guide for selection of respirators for some common jobs. However, Table 11.1 may be of assistance to those involved in asbestos removal. It should not necessarily be assumed that the data given is finite and assessment of the levels should be carried out by air sampling if there is any doubt. The levels quoted are drawn from experience in the work. Where there is doubt of the type of asbestos, crocidolite or amosite should be assumed.

Table 11.1

Recommended RPE for asbestos removal

Job	Asbestiform fibre concentration fibres/ml	Equipment necessary
Short sampling operations		
Simple enclosure erection	0-2	Any approved respirator
Clearance sampling		
Inspection		

Sampling in dusty areas		
Enclosure erection in dusty areas	0-4	Approved respirators other than half mask
Extensive sampling on friable materials Enclosure work in bad areas	4-20	Any approved high-efficiency respirator
Controlled wet stripping where effectively wetted	0-180	Any approved high-efficiency respirator except visors and half masks
Dry stripping or ineffective wet stripping	180-500	Any approved positive powered respirator. No others acceptable
Dry stripping in confined areas	500+	Some high-efficiency positive presssure respirators (check types), blouses and suits
Removal of asbestos sheet materials	0-25	Any approved high-efficiency respirator
Removal of asbestos cement	0-2	Any approved respirator

Personal protective clothing

Footwear

Footwear for use in the working enclosure should be capable of being cleaned of fibres and debris with no cracks or seams to collect contamination. The soles should be relatively smooth so as not to collect asbestos debris from the floor. Wellington boots, which can be washed clean before removal from the area, are the usual working footwear. Transit footwear must be provided where the decontamination facility is remote from the work area. It should conform to the same basic requirements.

Gloves

Gloves should be worn. They will normally be coated and should be tight at the wrists and long enough to be covered by the sleeve of the coverall.

Coveralls

Work in the asbestos enclosure should be carried out wearing coveralls including a hood. They should be elasticated at the wrist and ankles and have no pockets. The material should be impermeable to asbestos fibres.

When in use, the hood should be worn outside the RPE and pulled down to meet the rim of the facepiece. Wristbands should be outside the glove and legs outside the footwear.

Coveralls are available in a number of materials: polycotton, nylon, breathable plastics which are re-usable, as well as paper and other disposables.

For re-use, dirty coveralls should be placed in a water-soluble bag and then in a polythene bag, sealed and labelled in accordance with the regulations. Laundering should be carried out only at a laundry equipped for the purpose; by workers trained to handle the contaminated materials, and with procedures to allow for a dirty reception area, laundering and clean despatch areas. Monitoring should be undertaken and decontamination facilities provided for those working with the contaminated clothing. Whilst potential airborne contamination is limited by the use of the water soluble bag, it cannot be guaranteed that asbestiform fibres will not be released once the clothes have been washed. Fibre release can occur during the drying and repacking stages dependent on the efficiency of washing.

The effluent water from washing should be filtered to prevent loss of asbestos to the sewer and the air from drying should be filtered to prevent loss of fibres with the exhaust.

Disposable coveralls should be bagged and disposed of with the general asbestos waste.

Coveralls made from breathable plastics can be worn into the showers or washed off in a suitable area and thus decontaminated for re-use. Care is necessary and it must not be assumed that because they have been washed off there will be no residue to become airborne once they are dry.

Underwear

In many situations, the working conditions require that some clothing is worn under the protective coveralls. Unless this is disposable such underwear must be regarded as contaminated and treated as such. It should be laundered in a similar manner to the coveralls and separately from the more contaminated outer wear.

Associated equipment

Air extraction equipment 'negative pressure units'

Legislation demands that air extraction and negative pressure working are provided when working with asbestos. This is particularly so with insulation and coatings and is also necessary when working with asbestos insulation board and most asbestos cement products when inside buildings.

The requirement has not yet been the subject of guidance notes issued to help contractors in the stripping field. This section will therefore attempt to explain some of the basic aspects of the use and application of the equipment.

The term 'negative pressure' has become part of the jargon of the industry but does not fully define the purpose of air extraction from an asbestos enclosure.

The main concept of negative pressure is understood; less clear is the aspect of air extraction. Negative pressure provides a lower pressure inside the work area than outside. Thus if there are points of leakage, such leaks will be inwards rather than outwards and dust will be retained within the enclosure. Air extraction provides movement of air within the enclosure and removes airborne dust which is collected in the filtration unit of the ventilation equipment. The greater the volume of air extracted, the more airborne dust will be drawn from the enclosure atmosphere and the greater the number of air changes will be provided.

Without inward leakage in some manner the enclosure could collapse due to the fan suction. Therefore, the system must be designed for this criterion.

Negative pressure levels can be affected by outside influences such as wind, warm air rising from heated surfaces inside the work area and by the design of airlock systems.

Experience has shown that the differential between the external and internal pressures should be not less than 0.5 inches water gauge to eliminate leakage of asbestos dust from the work area.

Exhaust ventilation is required not only to achieve the negative pressure, but to provide the minimum practical fibre levels within the working area, even though the operatives are equipped with RPE. In most cases the atmosphere becomes warm and humid which adversely affects the working efficiency.

Asbestos stripping operations do not allow the ideal situation for calculation of air movement as air changes per hour, but as far as possible, the extraction rate of the fan should allow for 8-10 times the enclosure volume with a flow from one end to the other at approximately 30 litres per minute. In warm enclosures the rate fan size should be increased to take account of the increased temperatures and expansion of the air. Fan ratings are given at normal temperature and pressure. Air extraction equipment which is in general use consists of two units connected with flexible hosing. The filter box should be connected to a suitable point of the enclosure by a flange facing which can accept a pre-filter changeable from inside the work area. This will collect the gross material produced by the removal work and protect and prolong the life of the HEPA (high-efficiency particle arrestor) filter which provides effective removal; (99.997 per cent) of the micron-sized airborne asbestos fibres.

Air is drawn through the filtration unit by a suction fan and is usually exhausted outside the building via flexible hosing. The fan is designed so that consistent flow and pressure differential is maintained as the filters become loaded with dust.

Various arrangements can be provided to increase or decrease the flow to match requirements. Most suppliers provide a range of units for different design flows, either with variable speed fans or dampers to give reduced flow below the unit design level. The damper system has a distinct advantage over the variable speed fan, although both are available separately or in combination.

Vacuum cleaning

Cleaning units are generally industrial versions of the domestic cylinder vacuum cleaner. However, they are required to be fitted with a filter system of similar efficiency to that used for the negative-pressure air extraction units. The filters are required to be operated under negative pressure, i.e. before the extraction fan, and the equipment is available under the generic term of Type H vacuum cleaning equipment.

Chapter 12

HANDLING
AND DISPOSAL
OF ASBESTOS WASTE

The procedures previously discussed will, if carried out correctly, ensure that minimal risk is caused to workers and others during removal operations. However, the controls do not stop at that point. Asbestos waste must be collected, transported and disposed to ensure that there is no risk in those circumstances.

Work site

Waste and debris should be collected into bags or other receptacles as it is produced within the work area. This will prevent spread of the material around the work area and limit evolution of dust. Insulation waste should be collected and not allowed to build up on the floor of the work area. Sheet materials should as far as possible be removed whole, stacked and wrapped for disposal. Asbestos cement sheeting removed in external work should be removed whole and stored carefully for removal. Broken sheets should be wetted down and the pieces collected into bags or other containers to prevent crushing by machinery or foot traffic.

Waste should be placed in impermeable and dust-tight bags or containers. Prior to disposal it should be double-bagged or sealed and placed into a secure container or skip for transport.

The double-bag procedure requires that if polythene bags are used the inner bag should be red and should be manufactured from extruded material – low density polythene, which does not contain any material which has been previously extruded. The bag should be at least 125 microns (500 gauge) thick and should comply with BS 4932. It should be labelled to indicate its contents. The outer bag is generally of clear polythene and should be of similar specification and labelling or allow the label on the inner bag to be easily readable.

In the double-bagging procedure, once filled, the first bag should be sealed and then cleaned before being moved into the dirty airlock where it will be placed inside a second bag. This will itself be sealed and should also be cleaned before it is moved through the rest of the airlock chain prior to disposal. Sufficient red and clear bags should be provided in the work area and airlock to contain the anticipated quantity of waste.

On large projects it is possible to use drums in place of bags for the removal and storage of asbestos waste. In this application the waste is mixed with resin bonding, or possibly cement, and compressed into drums which are then sealed for disposal following a decontamination process through the airlocks.

All waste disposal bags or other receptacles should be labelled in accordance with the requirements set out later.

Following decontamination bags or containers should be placed in secure skips for transport and disposal.

Legal requirements of disposal

The Control of Pollution (Special Waste) Regulations 1980 define requirements for the movement of special wastes, including most types of waste asbestos, especially insulation and coatings and any waste containing crocidolite. They cover by inference if not specifically, broken asbestos insulation board or asbestos cement products.

Consignment note

These regulations place an obligation on the waste producer, carrier and disposer. The producer, the asbestos removal contractor, must complete the 'Consignment Note for Carriage and Disposal of Hazardous Wastes' and follow the procedures required by the regulations. The consignment note is frequently known as the 'section 17 form' and can be obtained from the hazardous waste unit of the local authority in whose jurisdiction the waste is to be disposed. In practice the disposal contractor who is to receive the waste will usually keep a stock of the forms for his clients.

Table 12.1

Section 17 form

County Council—Waste Disposal Branch— Tel. No.	SERIAL No.
	W.D.A. D.H. No.
CONSIGNMENT NOTE FOR THE CARRIAGE & DISPOSAL OF HAZARDOUS WASTES (Regulation 4 of Section 17—Control of Pollution Act 1974)	PRENOTIFICATION COPY

Producer's Certificate A

(1) The material described in B is to be collected from ....
....

and (2) taken to ....
....

Name .... Address of firm if different from (1)

Signed ....

Position ....

On behalf of ....

Telephone ....

Date .... Estimated date of collection ....

Description of the Waste B

(1) General description and physical nature of waste

(2) Relevant chemical and biological components and maximum concentrations

(3) Quantity of waste and size, type and number of containers .

(4) Process(es) from which waste originated.

Carrier's Collection Certificate C

I certify that I collected the consignment of waste and that the information given in A(1) & (2) and B(1) & (3) is correct, subject to any amendment listed in this space or in box below*

I collected this consignment on .... at .... hours ....

Signed .... On behalf of ....

Name .... Address ....

Vehicle Registration No. ....

Date .... Telephone No. ....

Producer's Collection Certificate D

I certify that the information given in B & C is correct and that the carrier was advised of appropriate precautionary measures.

Signed .... Name ....

Telephone No. .... Date. ....

Disposer's Certificate E

I certify that Waste Disposal Licence No. .... issued by Kent County Council, authorises the treatment/disposal at this facility of the waste described in B (and as amended where necessary at C). Name and address of facility. ....

This waste was delivered in vehicle (Reg. No.) .... at .... hours

on (date).. and the carrier gave his name as ....

on behalf of .... Proper instructions were given that the waste should

be taken to .... (location on site as Grid Reference)

Signed .... Name .... Position ....

Date .... On behalf of ....

* For use by Producer/ Carrier/ Disposer

00003471

The form, as shown in Table 12.1, is provided in multiple, no carbon copies required.

The complete consignment note comprises the following six copies.

Pre-notification copy

The producer of the waste must complete parts A and B and forward them to the waste disposal authority in whose area the waste is to be disposed. At least three clear days' notice are required for this notification to be received.

The remaining five copies should then be made available to the site from which the waste is to be collected.

Producer's copy – Blue

Producers' copy – Green

When the load is collected, the driver will sign part C and the producer will sign part D. The blue and green copies will then be retained by the producer and the remaining three taken by the driver. The producer should then forward the blue copy to the waste disposal authority in whose area he operates. The green copy should be retained in his records – it will be checked periodically by the waste disposal authority.

Carrier's copy – Orange

This will be presented by the driver when he arrives at the disposal site and must be signed before the waste is discharged. The driver will then retain the carrier's copy. The orange copy must be kept in the carrier's records. The remaining copies will be kept by the disposal site.

Producer's WDA copy – Yellow

The disposal site will forward the yellow copy to the waste disposal authority in whose area the producer operates. This will be checked against the blue copy originally sent by the producer to the same waste disposal authority.

Disposal site record copy – Pink

This will be held by the disposal site in its records.

The various copies of the consignment note must be retained by the recipients for at least two years.

Wherever possible, asbestos waste should be kept separate from other materials. If mixed loads are prepared by the removal contractor metal sections could cause rupture of the waste bags with consequent risks of emission of dust during the tipping operation. There is also the temptation to salvage metals from the load which can cause fibre release.

Transport of asbestos waste

Containers and skips

The carrier of the asbestos waste must provide suitable vehicles for the duty and a specially designed container or skip should be considered.

This should be sufficiently strong to withstand impact during a traffic accident and, in the case of skips, should be fabricated from steel sheeting at least 3mm thick on a steel framework. Walk-in doors enable every part of the unit to be reached with ease during loading to avoid throwing the bags. All access points to the skip must be lockable, but padlocks are not recommended because keys can be lost and it is too easy to cut the chain or the padlock itself to gain access. The inside surfaces of the skip should be smooth with no obvious points where dust and debris can collect in order to allow for easy cleaning in the event of asbestos contaminations. All containers used for the carriage of 500 kilograms or more of asbestos waste are required to display statutory 'dangerous substance markings' which must be clearly visible to other road users.

Training and instruction

Formal training and instruction should be given by the carrier to all drivers in his employ who may transport hazardous waste.

Training and instruction records should be kept and should be available to the driver. All drivers should be made aware of the nature and hazards relating to the waste and action to be taken in emergencies as well as their statutory duties under the various legislation.

The following is a checklist of action to be taken:

1   Before leaving the depot to work check:

- dangerous substance labels
- adequate personal protective clothing, respirators, boots and gloves for all persons with the vehicle.

2   The waste has been correctly loaded into the skip when collecting.

3   The consignment note has been completed by the producer of the waste and that due pre-notification has been given to the hazardous waste unit in whose area the waste will be disposed.

4   The waste is transported only to the pre-arranged licensed tip for disposal and that on arrival the consignment note is completed and the gold copy of the note is retained.

5   Careful discharge of the waste from the skip or container under the direction of the tip operator and that covering is being carried out. There is no residue of asbestos left in the skip; if necessary, wash out. On completion of the discharge remove or cover the dangerous substances labels.

6   Return to the base and hand in the consignment note copies. OR, if collecting a further consignment, ensure that the consignment documentation for the load discharged is kept separate from that of others to be collected.

7   Whilst loaded, the vehicle should be either parked in a safe place or if in transit, under the close supervision of a competent person.

8   The driver must be able to produce any documents relating to the load on request by a police officer or Department of Transport examiner.

The above checks, if correctly carried out, should avoid the need for emergency actions. The tip operation will be geared to cope with the eventualities of spillage or damaged bags and the transporting principles should thereby avoid accidental spillage in transit.

However, it is important that the driver and any assistants should understand and rehearse the emergency procedure in event of release of asbestos waste during transit.

The first and foremost requirement must be to contain the spillage and prevent the spread of asbestos fibres to the atmosphere while collection and removal is organized. Personal protective equipment must be worn and the spillage should be covered with a plastic sheet or polythene, with weighted seals at the edges if practical. If not, a spray damping will avoid windblown spread whilst further action is being taken. The general public should be kept away from the area by warning ropes, etc.

The incident should be reported to the emergency services for record or assistance.

Small amounts of asbestos may be vacuumed up but larger quantities can require the full procedure involving enclosure, airlocks, etc.

Disposal site

All waste disposal sites which receive asbestos must be licensed to do so by the relevant waste disposal authority.

A licence to dispose of asbestos on a landfill site will be issued under the Control of Pollution Act 1974. It will impose appropriate conditions to cover health and safety as well as the control of water pollution. This does not however mean that regulations relating to asbestos can be ignored. These are covered under the Health and Safety at Work etc. Act 1974 and its subsequent specific regulations relating to asbestos.

Disposal operators should use personal protective equipment when off-loading and covering the deposited waste.

All asbestos waste should be deposited at the foot of the working face of the landfill site and the method of work should be such as to avoid dispersion of fibres and dust. All notifiable asbestos waste should be covered immediately with earth or other non-hazardous waste. Asbestos cement sheet, or similar materials where the asbestos is bonded, should be covered before work is stopped for the day.

The top, sides or face of the deposited asbestos should be covered with at least 0.5m excluding a lesser requirement for an end-of-day cover between layers. The final layer of waste in any area should be covered by at least 2m at the surface or flanks of that layer.

To allow for the possibility of re-excavation of a landfill site in which significant quantities of asbestos waste have been deposited it is essential that proper records are maintained by the site operator showing the position, quantities and depths of the deposit.

The drainage characteristics of the landfill site should not allow wash out of asbestos fibres which could pollute any water course and thus create an environmental hazard.

Labelling of asbestos wastes and waste carrying vehicles

The following regulations apply to labelling:

> Control of Pollution (Special Waste) Regulations 1980;
> Classification, Packaging and Labelling of Dangerous Substances Regulations 1984;
> Road Traffic (Carriage of Dangerous Substances in Packages) Regulations 1986.

Under the 1980 regulations loads of 500 kilograms or more of notifiable asbestos waste must display the statutory 'dangerous substances markings' when in transit. These are orange coloured plates with a black border.

The 1986 regulations provide for the labelling of such dangerous substances including asbestos waste during the production and transport of the materials.

Any container or receptacle, including polythene bags, which is used for storage or conveyance or disposal of asbestos waste must be labelled with the name and address of the producer, the contents of the receptacle, the possible risks and safety precautions.

The industry has developed a standardized label for this which is now available in printed form, or with a self-adhesive backing for use with asbestos in sheet form (see Figure 12.1).

Figure 12.1 *Warning label for asbestos waste*

Administration, control and monitoring of disposal

The waste disposal contractor/transporter of asbestos waste must maintain records of equipment and operation.

In view of the possible build-up of opinion against the transport and disposal of asbestos wastes and the potential for environmental hazard, the landfill site operator should consider environmental monitoring. This would take place at or around the disposal workface and the boundaries of the site. The results, carried out by independent laboratories will carry some weight should there be any argument on the environmental safety of the operation. Furthermore the results will maintain a check on operator routine and worker exposure as required by the Control of Asbestos at Work Regulations.

Bibliography

Regulations and Approved Codes of Practice

Asbestos Regulations 1969
Health and Safety at Work etc. Act 1974
Control of Pollution Act 1974
Asbestos (Licensing) Regulations 1985
Asbestos (Prohibition) Regulations 1985
Asbestos Products (Safety) Regulations 1985
Classification, Packaging and Labelling of Dangerous Substances
   Regulations 1984
Control of Asbestos at Work Regulations 1987
ACOP Work with asbestos insulation and asbestos coatings,
   revised February 1985
ACOP Control of asbestos at work 1988
ACOP Work with asbestos insulation, asbestos coatings and
   asbestos insulating board 1988
Asbestosis Research Council (Technical Note C)
Health and Safety Executive Guidance Notes:

EH10	Asbestos – Control Limits Measurement of Airborne Dust Concentration and Assessment of Control Measures revised (1988)
EH35	Probable Asbestos Dust Concentrations at Construction Processes (1984)
EH36	Work with Asbestos Cement (1984)
EH37	Work with Asbestos Insulating Board (1984)

EH41	Respiratory Protective Equipment for Use Against Asbestos (1985)
EH47	Provisional use on maintenance of hygiene facilities for work with asbestos insulation and coatings (1986)
GH5	Entry into confined spaces
GS29	Parts 1,2,3,4 Health and Safety in Demolition Work (1984/5)
MDHS39	Asbestos Fibres in Air, Determination of Personal Exposure by the European Reference version of the membrane filter method 1984 (revised 1988)

Miscellaneous

Department of the Environment:
Asbestos Materials in Buildings (1983)
Asbestos Waste – Technical Memorandum on Arising and Disposal including a Code of Practice (1979)
Certificate of Approval (Respiratory Protective Equipment F2486 (annual)
Doll, R. and Peto, J., *Effects on Health of Exposure to Asbestos,* 1985

Appendix: 'The Asbestos Company' – Code of Practice for Work with Asbestos Insulation, Asbestos Coatings and Asbestos Insulating Board

Foreword

This document is not intended to replace any regulatory, guidance or instruction material relating to health and safety, but is intended purely as a code of practice to be followed by the company and its employees. As such, it will assist in maintaining the high standard of performance we are known to be able to produce. It is intended to be used to complement safety policy and training manuals issued by the company.

The company will always strive to improve upon its present performance, be it in equipment, procedures or administration of asbestos projects.

From time to time this code of practice will be updated to take account of such improvements or modified regulations or guidance.

Signed: _____

      Director

Introduction

Asbestos is an emotive subject. It has been stated that one minute particle entering the body may be sufficient to trigger off the diseases associated with exposure to asbestos dust in those who are susceptible.

The purpose of this code of practice is to provide guidance and advice on safe systems of work with asbestos on all sites at which the company is employed.

Working to this code of practice should ensure that asbestos removal works are carried out in accordance with current legislation, guidance notes and sound practice as interpreted by the authorities, without endangering the health and safety of those persons directly concerned with the work and others who may be affected by acts or omissions in the furtherance of such works.

Relevant regulation and guidance

The Code of Practice should be considered as the minimum applicable standard and complementary to:

1   The Health and Safety at Work etc Act 1974
2   The Public Health Act 1936
3   The Asbestos (Licensing) Regulations 1983
4   The Control of Pollution Act 1974
5   The Control of Pollution (Special Waste) Regulations 1980
6   The Factories Act 1961
7   The Construction Industry Regulations 1985
8   The Asbestos (Prohibition) Regulations 1985
    Codes of Practice and guidance notes. nos. EH35, EH36, EH37, EH41, EH47, EH10.
9   Control of Asbestos at Work Regulations 1987

In all cases, compliance with the latest requirements of the relevant statutory instruments, codes of practice and guidance information, including the above, will be required as a minimum standard. The Control of Asbestos at Work Regulations came into effect on March 1 1988. They replace the Asbestos Regulations 1969 and extend the control to other spheres in conjunction with the Health and Safety at Work etc. Act 1974.

General

It is not intended that this code of practice should necessarily cover work involving products such as asbestos cement, floor tiles containing asbestos or asbestos board which may have thermal or acoustic properties incidental to their main functions. However, where the situation, location or client code of practice requires, the procedures as set down will apply to such work in addition to that for which this code of practice is specifically prepared.

It is emphasized that this document is therefore complementary to any specific requirements of any client.

The contents of this document should provide a basis for a safe system of work which will enhance the safety of our employees and members of the public who may be affected by our employees' acts or omissions in the furtherance of work with asbestos materials.

It is essential that all persons working with asbestos materials are provided with adequate information, instruction, training and supervision, so that they are aware of:

hazards connected with the work;
measures necessary to eliminate possible risk;
training and proficiency in the safe systems of work;
safe use and maintenance of equipment,

and are supervised in such a way as to ensure that they comply with the requirements of safety regulations and codes of practice at all times.

Control limits and guidance for airborne asbestos dust

The Guidance Note EH10 issued by the Health and Safety Executive provides information on asbestos control limits and measurement of airborne dust concentrations. This sets out the control limits agreed by the Health and Safety Commission, effective from 1 August 1984.

The control limits for occupationally exposed persons (e.g. asbestos strippers) are:

| For dust consisting of or containing any crocidolite or amosite | 0.2 fibres/ml when measured as a time weighted average over any four (4) hour period |
| For dust consisting of or containing any other types of asbestos but not crocidolite or amosite | 0.5 fibres/ml when measured as a time weighted average over any four (4) hour period |

However, the control limits as set out above *do not* represent safe levels which, once attained, make further improvements in dust control unnecessary. They represent the upper limits of permitted exposure, as determined by personal sampling techniques.

Unless otherwise previously agreed in writing, the company will adopt the following procedure:

All work with asbestos will assume that the control limits are exceeded. Operatives will wear full protective equipment and clothing until such time as it is proved unnecessary by air monitoring.

For air tests outside the working area and in the clean areas of decontamination facilities, a determination of airborne fibres of greater than 0.01 fibres/ml will result in corrective measures being undertaken.

If determinations above 0.02 fibres/ml are obtained then all work will stop until the cause has been determined and corrected and the count reduced to less than 0.01 fibres/ml.

All air monitoring on behalf of the company will be carried out by a suitably qualified competent person totally independent of the company.

General safety requirements

When work on asbestos-based materials is being undertaken it is essential to safeguard the health and safety of visitors or any other persons that may be affected by act or omission of our employees during the period of work. This applies whether the work being undertaken is sampling, removal or treatment of asbestos-based materials.

It is the duty of the company to provide appropriate protective clothing and respiratory equipment for any authorized visitors who may need to visit the work area in which work on asbestos-based materials is being undertaken.

The degree of protection required will clearly be dependent upon the level of risk, e.g. persons expected to enter the working area will require the same degree of protection as provided for the operatives working in the same area whilst those remaining outside will require, if any, a lower level of protection.

All personnel who work with or are likely to come into contact with asbestos as part of their routine duties, will be medically examined to ensure their fitness to carry out work. Medical examinations will be repeated at regular intervals and the details recorded in a register.

All personnel involved in any aspect of work within the terms of reference of this code of practice will be given training relevant to their responsibilities. This training and the maintenance of working practices and standards will be the responsibility of a designated member of the company management team.

We should also try to ensure that any authorized person entering the enclosed working area is medically fit, and able to wear the necessary protective clothing required.

Bulk sampling

Before work is commenced on the removal or treatment of materials containing asbestos, it is essential that the type and condition of asbestos be determined. The procedures set out below should provide practical guidance on safe methods of taking, collecting and submitting asbestos material samples. Where possible this work will normally be undertaken by an independent analytical laboratory service acting on our behalf. Where this is not possible, sampling will be undertaken only by persons who have been adequately trained.

Taking of samples

It is important to ensure that samples are truly representative of the materials involved. In the case of loose or friable insulation materials the full depth of material should be sampled, if necessary, at more than one point.

Precautions to be taken:

1   All persons not directly involved in the sampling should be excluded from the area. Warning notices 'Asbestos sampling, keep clear' should be posted around the perimeter of the area. Notices must be printed and clearly visible.

2   Any equipment, machinery, furnishings or household goods which might become contaminated during the sampling operation should be removed or protected, as necessary.

3   The person taking the sample must be adequately protected to a level appropriate to the work to be carried out. In some circumstances, full protective clothing will be necessary, e.g. where there is a risk of clothing becoming contaminated due to the location of the materials in particularly confined or restricted areas such as ducts, or where there is already a concentration or accumulation of dust.

4   Samples will be taken in such a way as to keep to a minimum disturbance to the sampled materials. Hand tools as opposed to power tools, and sharp instruments rather than sawing instruments will be used to obtain samples.

5   After sampling, the sampling point must be re-sealed, any small quantity of dust that is apparent will be collected on a damp cloth or other suitable material which is then placed into a polythene bag. This bag and its contents are then placed into another polythene bag, in compliance with the double-bag requirement, and carefully disposed of in a correct manner with other asbestos waste to an approved disposal site.

6   Any areas of suspected asbestos material damaged by sampling must be rendered temporarily safe, e.g. by sealing or wrapping until the results of the tests are known.

Persons who normally work in the area will, where appropriate, be reassured as to their safety on re-occupation. Air tests may be necessary to achieve this reassurance.

Each sample taken must be double wrapped within two stout self-sealing impervious polythene bags or other suitable storage container.

The sample submitted should be clearly labelled with the following information:
- asbestos sample;
- client name;
- site of origin;
- location on site;
- date;
- person taking sample;
- other information as necessary, such as a sketch of the area which locates the samples taken.

Asbestos removal (stripping)

Work at any particular site may involve a single or combination of methods of removal. The methods of work and control will be such as to ensure that, as far as practical, asbestos dust shall be confined within the designated working area.

Stripping methods may be generally defined as follows:

- dry stripping;
- wet stripping;
- stripping by high-pressure water jets.

All methods of stripping should be discussed with the client and his representatives who must be fully aware of what is involved in the method selected.

Before any project starts the method of work and procedures will be determined and a written statement prepared. This will be specific for the particular location and will be issued to the Health and Safety Executive, client, site staff and independent analyst for their information. Site staff will not vary from the written procedures without authority.

Dry stripping

This technique involves the removal of asbestos materials from surfaces without the use of water or other agents to reduce dust. The following points should be considered:

1 Because a high level of asbestos dust concentration is created, a correspondingly high standard of approved positive pressure respiratory protective equipment and protective clothing will be necessary.
2 The work area enclosure will need to be a very high standard of construction to prevent the escape of asbestos dust. The enclosure will be checked by filling with smoke to test the integrity of the seals before any work commences. Visual checks will also be made prior to any re-commencement of work following meal and shift breaks.
3 Operatives will require a high degree of training for the work and safety precautions.
4 The safety officer will give instructions of a safe system of work and a method statement should be posted adjacent to the airlock system.
5 The site foreman/manager will exercise close supervision of control of waste materials.
6 The site supervisor will ensure that operatives maintain respiratory protective equipment in good condition as instructed during training.
7 Operatives will be supervised in the use of vacuum equipment and negative air movement equipment to reduce dust levels at source.
8 All stripped surfaces, or surfaces likely to have been contaminated, will be treated with a sealant to ensure that no asbestos fibres are released by subsequent work.
9 The filtration equipment (negative pressure units) of a size suitable to the work area (as called for by the method statement, decided by supervisor and/or client controlling officer) will be installed as part of the enclosure operation. The size should provide a minimum of eight air changes per hour. This equipment will create a negative pressure in the enclosure which serves two purposes: (*a*) to reduce dust

levels, and (*b*) to reduce the risk of dust escaping from the enclosure.

10 Air filtration equipment must be fitted with high-efficiency particle arrestor (HEPA) filters to 99.997 per cent efficiency, and where possible, the extracted air should be vented to the outside atmosphere.

11 All waste (and contaminated debris) must be, as soon as is practical, placed into a regulation red polythene bag and sealed. The bag will be of not less than 500 gauge. No waste shall be allowed to remain unbagged at the end of a working day or shift.

12 The red bag must be cleaned on the outside before being moved into the airlock compartment nearest the working area, where it will be double-bagged using a regulation clear polythene bag.

13 The outer clear bag will then be cleaned before being passed out from the same airlock for disposal to a skip, which will be kept locked at all times when not being loaded with waste.

The environment outside the enclosure will be monitored during the stripping operation by an independent analyst to ensure that airborne fibre concentration is maintained well below the appropriate control limits and this company's action limits. The frequency of such monitoring will depend on local conditions, but an analyst will be available on call at all times when asbestos removal work is being carried out.

On completion of asbestos removal, the work area will be subject to a vigorous inspection generally by an independent analyst/inspector, prior to the taking of air samples to establish airborne fibre concentration. No clearance will be given unless the inspection is satisfactory with no visible residual asbestos and the airtests have fibre counts of less than 0.01 fibres/ml when taken following disturbance in the work area.

Wet stripping

Great care should be taken during the setting up of the enclosure for the wet stripping procedure.

1   The site supervisor must personally ensure that all electrical equipment in the working area is safely isolated by a responsible person from the client personnel, e.g. a lock-off system carried out by a competent person as defined in regulations made under the Factories Act 1961. He must also ensure that steps are taken to prevent the ingress of water or other liquids into the electrical system.

When removal work is completed and air monitoring clearance given, the site supervisor must ensure that the electrical system has been checked before supply is restored.

2   A permit-to-work system will be applied before work commences.

3   Removal of metal or other non-asbestos cladding in order to obtain access to the asbestos materials will be carried out carefully. The surfaces of the cladding will be cleaned with vacuum cleaners and/or washed with water and sealed with a PVA sealing agent before they are removed from the work area.

4   At the commencement of work, but before any stripping takes place, the asbestos material will be thoroughly soaked with water using a wetting agent such as common detergent.

5   The soaked material will then be removed in sections, placed immediately in polythene bags and sealed. They will then be removed from the work area to the removal train, washed, placed in a second clear bag and sealed for disposal.

6   Slurry must be removed immediately and not allowed to dry on surfaces.

7   No re-insulation work or sealing work will be undertaken until removal work has been completed and full inspections and clearance tests have certified the area clear for use.

8   Where wet stripping or wet cleaning has been carried out, the area and surfaces must be completely dry before air clearance tests are taken.

High-pressure water jet stripping

This is probably the least used method of asbestos removal. It is a highly specialized technique using pressure of 2000 pounds per square inch or more.

The pressure jet system is usually restricted to situations where, because of difficulty in obtaining direct access to sprayed coatings, other techniques are not efficient; also on larger areas where consideration can be given to the collection and disposal of water residue. However, if correctly planned and controlled the procedure can be very effective.

Eye protection must be worn at all times during this operation. See Protection of Eyes Regulations 1974. RPE must meet this requirement. The following points must be considered:

1 Pre-soaking is required before water jetting commences to prevent the jet dislodging asbestos material before it is thoroughly wet.

2 Ear protection must be worn if noise levels from high-pressure water jets exceed 105 DBA.

3 The jet can inflict serious injury by impact, cutting or penetration of the skin. Safety clothing as provided must be worn. This technique will only be undertaken by trained personnel under the immediate control of a competent supervisor.

4 Warning notices – 'Danger High Pressure Jetting' – must be displayed at strategic positions and in sufficient numbers outside the working area to prevent unauthorized entry.

5 Water-jetting equipment should be properly maintained with records available for inspection at head office.

6 The jet will be controlled by a dead mans control valve which, when released, prevents the delivery of high pressure water from the appliance. This safety device must never be tied back to provide continuous flow.

7 This method will only be used where there is no electrical supply or where equipment and supply are isolated and pronounced safe to work by a competent person and where a specific permit to work is so issued. Additional precautions will be taken by the site supervisor to ensure that electrical power cannot be restored accidentally during the period of these works.

8   Water must be prevented from penetrating electrical equipment or conductors in the working areas.

9   On completion of the work the site will be inspected to ensure that it is safe to restore the electrical supply.

10 Suitable waterproof protective clothing, approved respiratory protection and ear defenders will be supplied and must be worn.

11 Slurry will be collected and treated as contaminated waste and disposed of accordingly.

12 Water must be filtered effectively before entry to drainage systems.

Control of waste asbestos

The following are procedures for dealing with asbestos waste:

1   The company provides polythene bags of two colours which meet statutory requirements including all warning notices, information and company name and address. The bags are for the disposal of asbestos waste and must only be used for this purpose.

2   All waste materials must be transferred from surfaces to red bags (of which a supply will be in the work area) and sealed as soon as is practical.

3   The outside of each red bag must be cleaned immediately prior to its removal from the work area to the nearest airlock compartment.

4   A supply of clear bags will be provided in the airlock compartment nearest the work area.

5   The cleaned red bag will be placed in a clear bag, and the clear bag sealed.

6   The clear bag will be cleaned before it is removed.

7   Any bags not carrying the required information must be marked with a self adhesive label before being placed in a lockable skip. The site supervisor will hold a supply of these labels.

8   All transportation and disposal of asbestos waste will comply with the relevant legislation, in particular, section 17 of the Control of Pollution Act and the Transport of Hazardous Waste Regulations.

The site supervisor will ensure that under no circumstances will any asbestos waste material remain on the floor of the work area after the working day.

All asbestos waste sacks and/or labels are printed to comply with current regulations, legislation and latest guidance notes.

Disposal and transportation of asbestos waste

Asbestos waste is covered by the Control of Pollution (Special Waste) Regulations 1980 which make asbestos a 'notifiable' material. The local authority in whose area the waste is being disposed must be informed by a manager or person of higher position in the company.

Waste asbestos must be disposed of at a licensed tip.

Waste asbestos or asbestos contaminated waste must be separated from all other waste and placed in separate skips.

Asbestos waste must be transported in an approved vehicle when being moved from a minor works site to a sited skip. At all other times a licensed waste disposal company will be used.

Protective clothing and equipment

Respiratory protective equipment (RPE)

Any person who enters the airlock system and working area when removal works are in progress must be fully equipped so to do. Those persons taking samples or transporting waste bags to skips are likely to be exposed to concentrations of asbestos in excess of 0.01f/ml, and must wear the respiratory equipment and other personal safety equipment provided.

RPE will be of an approved type which conforms to the requirements of BS 4275 (1984) and the Health and Safety Executive Guidance Note EH-41

All company personnel required to use RPE will have received specific training as to its correct use, operation, care and maintenance. All such persons will have been examined by an appointed approved medical examiner.

The site supervisor will ensure that all personnel on site are in possession of the required RPE, and that the procedures laid down for maintenance, cleaning, disinfection and filter changing are followed.

All personnel who wear respiratory equipment will be clean shaven around the facial areas which come into contact with the equipment, i.e. no beards or sideburns.

Spare RPE units should be available on site from the site supervisor should any problems occur during removal operations. At least two sets for emergency use will also be maintained and available.

Maintenance of respiratory equipment

Each person using RPE is responsible for its maintenance and the site supervisor is responsible for that issued to visitors, etc.

At the end of each period of work users will:

- remove excess asbestos material from the exterior surfaces of the equipment using a vacuum cleaner and water, ensuring that cleaning does not affect the inhalation and exhalation valves;
- remove contaminated filters;
- wash and disinfect inside the face piece;
- check valves for correct function and wear;
- if fitted, place the battery on charge, and
- test RPE before re-use.

At least once per week, supervisors will:

- examine RPE for cracks, wear and deterioration of rubber and plastic parts;
- examine RPE for damage or wear to straps, hose, clips, buckles and valves, and
- check that the personal identification is visible.

Overalls

The usual form of protective clothing provided by the company consists of one-piece hooded overalls which can be securely fastened at the front, up to the neck, with elasticated wrist and ankle bands and void of pockets. They are made of polycotton, of a density which avoids penetration of fibres whether wet or dry and are disposable.

Overalls used in the working area will be *red* and will not be taken away from the work area, except in a sealed asbestos waste sack, as asbestos waste.

Overalls used in transit will be *white* and used only for transit. *No overalls will be worn, other than those supplied by the company.*

At the end of each working period red overalls should be vacuum cleaned in a clear area inside the work area adjacent to, and before entering, the airlock. This serves two purposes:

-   it prolongs the working life of overalls, and
-   it reduces contamination of airlock compartments.

Boots and footwear

Wellington boots are provided for each operative and must be worn in the work area. They will be worn inside the trouser leg of the overalls. No other footwear will be worn and the supervisor is responsible for ensuring compliance.

Gloves

Rubber gloves are provided by the company and will be worn by all operatives inside the work enclosure. They will be washed at the end of each period of work and left in the airlock compartment nearest the work area. Heavy duty gloves for rough work should be treated as asbestos waste at the end of the work period and disposed of in a sealed waste sack.

Vacuum and air extraction equipment

Vacuum and air extraction equipment is a very important part of our industry.

All apparatus must be fitted with a high efficiency (hepa) filtration system tested to at least BS 3928, 1969. In the case of vacuum-cleaning appliances, they are also manufactured, tested and certified to BS 5415, part 2, section 2.2, 1967, as in the fourth amendment, AM2 4570. The vacuum cleaner, known as a type H, is clearly marked: 'This appliance contains dust hazardous to health'. Emptying and maintenance operations including removal and renewal of dust collection bags will be carried out by authorized personnel, wearing suitable personal protection. Usually this will be the site supervisor. The cleaner must never be operated without the full filter system fitted.

The high efficiency filter containers fitted to vacuum and air extraction plant are clearly labelled: 'Asbestos dust, removal and renewal of filters to be carried out by authorized personnel only'.

Maintenance

Plant must be kept in efficient working order and good repair. The following is the minimum standard of maintenance to be adopted:

1 The plant will be inspected at the commencement of each working period and tested to ensure there are no leaks and that it functions in accordance with the manufacturer's specification and instructions. Change pre-filter.
2 A further in-depth inspection will be carried out once in every seven (7) days or at the end of a contract, with attention being paid to the internal workings and filters. The following work will be carried out only by persons wearing full personal protective equipment, who will normally be a site supervisor:
    - ensure that the pre-filters are removed safely;
    - vacuum out the filter container, avoiding contact with the absolute filter;

- examine the flexible hose or duct for leaks and internal cleanliness – if in doubt, seal the item inside an impervious container for disposal;
- examine the extractor motor for function and external defects and remove it from service if it is showing signs of deterioration;
- report any faults for remedial action to be taken.

3 A thorough examination and test will be carried out by a person specifically trained for the work, at least once every 6 months, normally at the manufacturer's premises.

Electrical equipment

Many clients use apparatus on a reduced voltage of 110 volts and it is therefore necessary to have in stock a supply of both 110 volts and 240 volts equipment. Extreme care must be taken when selecting equipment from stock for a specific contract. The site supervisor will be responsible that all equipment is as specified on the contract.

Plugs and sockets for the respective voltages differ, to conform to BS 196, 1961, and at no time should fittings be exchanged.

All maintenance will be carried out by a competent person appointed by the company.

Our equipment complies with all relevant regulations, British Standards (and kite marked accordingly) and meets the conditions of the 15th edition of the IEE Regulations as amended in 1983 and 1984.

Enclosure of the working area

Sheeting and tenting

A work area will have already been defined by survey and precontract meeting with the client before a removal crew arrive on site and will be specified in the method statement issued prior to setting up site.

When a site is very contaminated every effort must be made to reduce the risk of contaminating other areas not affected. This will be done by cleaning the floor of the work area before sealing work is started with vacuum equipment or a wet cleaning method, whichever is more practical, taking into consideration local conditions. Under no circumstances will dry brushing be undertaken as this will cause dust to rise. Warning signs must be posted, protective equipment worn and decontamination procedures followed.

The work area will be separated from the rest of the site by polythene sheet tenting (strengthened by timber batons where necessary) to 1000 gauge thickness (2 × 500 gauge may be used, because if one membrane is accidentally punctured, there is still another to prevent leakage whilst repairs are carried out).

Polyvinyl and foil tape of 2 or 3 inches width will be used to seal the edges of the polythene tenting.

Where a long underground duct is to be cleaned in stages, it may be more advantageous to build semi-permanent block walls with emergency escape doors built into them. These can be used again and will reduce set up time on the next phase and will stop recontamination between contracts.

Points to note are:

1 All external openings from the working area including doors, windows, ventilation openings, pipework and conduit through walls, will be sealed to prevent the escape of asbestos dust. Adhesive tape may be used where effective dust-tight joints are required. Expanding foam-mastics or mortar with tape covering can be used on larger holes.

2 Use existing partitions provided that they can be sealed to prevent the escape of asbestos dust.

3 Ensure that dust cannot escape at joints where surfaces interconnect.

4 Where it is not possible to use an existing partition, suitable impermeable sheeting should separate the working area from the remainder.

5 Where possible, air extraction/filtration plant will be located so as to provide air flow across the working area away from the airlock entry position.

The site supervisor will be responsible for ensuring that pre-filters are changed at the correct time by checking the negative pressure readings.

The negative pressure units will be operating continually once removal work has commenced until such time as air clearance tests are required.

The work enclosure must not under normal circumstances impede any means of escape from fire. Where this cannot be avoided, an alternative means of escape must be found. If this is not possible the local fire prevention officer or client's safety officer should be consulted.

The local fire brigade must be informed of all removal work taking place in tented areas, so that the correct equipment is readily available if fire or emergency should occur whilst stripping operations are in progress.

Monitoring of enclosure efficiency

On all sites where the removal of asbestos is undertaken, the Health and Safety Executive Guidance Note EH-10 will be adhered to.

Unless otherwise arranged by the client, the company will appoint an independent analyst to monitor inspections and air tests around the enclosure. This analyst will also, on some occasions, be employed as a supervising officer with full authority from the company to implement disciplinary procedures if necessary under S. 7 of the Health and Safety at Work etc. Act 1974.

The 'analyst' will:

- inspect the enclosure to ensure there are no openings;
- carry out some smoke tests to ensure the integrity of the seals;
- supervise any resealing and retesting should the first test fail;
- carry out a visual inspection of the enclosure before work starts each day;
- undertake continuous air monitoring outside the working enclosure and inside the airlock compartment from the

work area, after the first two hours of any work period.

- keep a record of all tests and inspections carried out on behalf of the company and post a copy of the records near to the airlock system for inspection.

If the analyst should at any time find airborne concentration outside the working area, or inside the airlock above figures set out in the guidelines, he must take the following course of action.

Where the readings are 0.01 fibre per ml:

- investigate cause of potential leak and correct it;
- carry out confirmatory short-interval sampling;
- advise personnel outside the working area to enable an internal inspection to be carried out.

If the reading reaches 0.02 fibre per ml:

- stop all work within the enclosure until the leak is found and corrected;
- carry out confirmatory short-interval sampling;
- prevent restart of work until concentration outside the work area has fallen below 0.01 fibre per ml.

Hygiene facilities

The airlock system will be cleaned at the end of each working day or when necessary as indicated by air test results showing contamination. The site supervisor will ensure that some person is detailed to this duty on a rota basis.

The decontamination unit which will be attached to or sited near the work area will contain three areas:

- changing area with lockers for storage of clean clothing, seat, mirror and washing;
- washing/shower area, hanger rails to hang clean RPE;
- changing area with lockers for work or transit clothing.

The decontamination unit will contain a heater to provide a reasonable air temperature, water heater for showers and washing, lights, an air ventilation system together with a negative air pressure unit giving correct air flow through high and low vents, and filtered drainage for effluent.

The site supervisor is responsible for the maintenance and working of the decontamination unit and must also ensure it is cleaned and disinfected daily after use.

Use of decontamination facilities

The procedure for entering the work area is as follows:

1 Enter clean area and remove all civilian domestic clothing or 'clean area' overalls. Don disposable underwear, if required. Secure all removed clothing into lockers provided. If necessary, test serviceable respirators and associated equipment.
2 Pass through showers directly into 'dirty' area. Ensure each door is closed before the next is opened.
3 Put on transit overalls, footwear, headgear and gloves if required.
4 Proceed to the working area entrance airlock system.
5 If in transit overalls and temporary footwear, remove this clothing and pass through into the 'dirty' airlock, dressed only in underwear and respirators.
6 In working area 'dirty' airlock, don working overalls and boots. Pass through airlock and enter working area.

When leaving the work area, as much asbestos fibre as possible should remain in the enclosure. Use the following procedure:

1 Vacuum off loose fibres from the outer covering of the protective clothing, including respirators. Avoid vacuum contact with respirator filters and face piece exhaust valve. Remove working overalls, boots and gloves. (If the decontamination unit is remote from the working area and transit overalls are in use, the working overalls will need to be secured adjacent to the working area inside the dirty airlock.)
2 Move into transit area entrance airlock and don transit overalls and footwear only. Do not remove respirator.

3   Remove protective clothing, except respirator and disposable underwear.
4   Enter central showers. Without removing the respirator, thoroughly shower the body, paying particular attention to the hair and fingernails. Towards the end of the shower process, remove the washed respirator and motor pack assembly, if fitted.

Medical surveillance

The Asbestos (Licensing) Regulations 1983 require persons working with asbestos insulation or coatings to be under medical surveillance. A certificate must be obtained to this effect at each medical examination.

The certificate can only be issued after a medical examination has been carried out by an employment medical advisor appointed under s. 56 (1) of the Health and Safety at Work etc. Act 1974, or a registered medical practitioner appointed in writing by the Health and Safety Executive.

The company is required to meet the cost of medical examinations of its employees for this purpose.

The examination will be repeated at least every two years and certificate records stored for at least four years.

The company will issue to each employee involved in asbestos removal a card verifying the fact that he has been examined. This card will carry a photograph of the person and may be issued for identification. The card remains the property of the company. Medical certificates are kept at head office but copies are available for inspection.

Records of examinations and inspections

Respiratory protection equipment

Date:

Site:

Equipment identification	Issued to	Face-piece	Positive pressure unit	Faults to be corrected	Action taken

Inspection carried out by:

Respiratory protection equipment record (weekly)

Equipment identification number:
(note facepiece and positive pressure unit must have the same number)

Issued to:

Supplier:

Date of inspection	Site	Defects noted	Checked by	Defects corrected date	Checked by

Air extraction equipment inspection sheet

Equipment identification number: Date:

To be completed weekly and forwarded to head office for record

1   *Check system resistance gauge* (acceptable reading)

    (*a*)   If too high, change pre-filter
    (*b*)   Check resistance gauge further
    (*c*)   If still too high, arrange for replacement HEPA filter

2   *Electrical supply*

    (*a*)   Cable
    (*b*)   Plug and attachments
    (*c*)   Switches

3   *Check HEPA filter unit*

    (*a*)   Are the tension bolts secure?   Yes/No
    (*b*)   Is the unit damaged in any way?   Yes/No
        If yes, specify

4   *Extractor*

    (*a*)   Is the unit operating effectively?   Yes/No
    (*b*)   Is the unit damaged?   Yes/No
    (*c*)   Is the airflow within limit   (   )?   Yes/No
    (*d*)   Results of air monitor test at exhaust

Checks carried out by:

Faults to be corrected (list)

Air extraction equipment record (weekly)

Equipment identification number:
Equipment serial number:
Equipment supplier:

Date of inspection	Site	Defects noted	Checked by	Defects corrected date	Checked

Vacuum cleaner record (weekly)

Equipment identification number:
Equipment serial number:
Equipment supplier:

Date of inspection	Site	Defects noted	Checked by	Defects corrected date	Checked

Decontamination facility inspection sheet (weekly)

Date: Site:

Unit identification number:

Comment   *Action required*

1   General structure
2   Clean section
3   Shower section
4   Dirty section

Inspection carried out by:

Faults to be corrected:

Decontamination facility record (weekly)

Unit identification number:

Date of inspection	Site	Defects noted	Checked by	Defects corrected date	Checked by

Medical surveillance record

Surname:	Date of commencement of this employment
Forenames:	
Birth surname	Previous exposure to Asbestos Yes/No

Address: If yes, year of first exposure:
                      Total years to date:

Date of birth: Previous employers where work was
                      carried out with asbestos

N.I. number: – list
NHS number:

Medical examination   Exposure record in this employment
record

Date	Remarks	Next due	Job description (include project)	Monitored exposure levels	RPE	Date

Index